HOW TO MANAGE CUSTOMER SERVICE

How to Manage Customer Service

Bernard Katz

Gower

Published by
Gower Publishing Company Limited,
Gower House,
Croft Road,
Aldershot,
Hants GU11 3HR,
England

British Library Cataloguing in Publication Data
Katz, Bernard
  How to manage customer service.
  1. Customer service—Management
  I. Title
  658.8′12   HF5415.5

ISBN 0–566–02631–7

Printed in Great Britain at the
University Press, Cambridge

Contents

Preface

Modern society has an increasing appetite for the skills of others. As a result, the service industries are growing. They affect many aspects of personal life. Some of the skills are technical, and are learned through prolonged, intensive training. Other skills are less demanding.

But aside from the technical complexity of the service, there are other, significant dimensions. Perhaps the most important is the marketing aspect. Expectation of service is an essential component of the purchase decision. The service function has to be researched, packaged, promoted, priced, distributed and sold in just the same way as the product itself. This book argues the case for the marketing mix to be updated from the traditional 'four Ps' to 'four Ps and an S' – Product, Price, Place, Promotion and Service. Service is a variable that management controls along with the four other 'P' variables.

Another important dimension is the behavioural aspect of supplying service. The employee behind a telephone providing timetable information gives service. So does the engineer repairing a faulty television set. How that service is given has a direct bearing on the survival and growth of the service supplier.

Good customer relations come from providing effective service. But giving that service is a continuous activity. It means being efficient, reliable, courteous, caring and professional every time. There is no provision for an 'off day'. Sometimes customers are angry. Occasionally they are unreasonable. Nevertheless, they are always customers requiring prompt, efficient service.

The book is aimed at managers who would like to treat service as a profit centre. It is also for those who have moved from service as a cost to the company, but seek to enhance the total service package. The book is in two parts. It covers planning for providing service, and the 'how' of giving that service.

There are checklists. There are rules for what to do and what to avoid. There are examples and discussion. There are training schedules. All are addressed to the manager. Many are intended for service personnel, through the manager.

Throughout, a question-and-answer format is adopted. A short list of 'test' questions precedes each chapter. These questions are then worked through in the text. The same questions, with answers, are given at the end of each chapter as a summary. Sometimes, when consistent with the subject, the questions that are asked are open-ended. In that situation, there is not really a 'test'. The reader's answer may differ from that given, but it is not necessarily wrong. The objective of the question-and-answer format is to signpost specific customer service problems and issues.

Within a framework of planning, good customer service is achieved through training. Training is a skill that applies to every kind of service. The reader is offered a training approach, because improving and practising those skills is the path to achieving and maintaining good customer relations.

Criticism, comments and suggestions in the field of customer service are invited by the author. Training problems experienced by managers in the United Kingdom and overseas are invited too: the solutions that are developed by dialogue provide new and useful teaching resources.

Bernard Katz
33 Wellesley Court
Maida Vale
LONDON W9 1RJ

Telex: 295441 BUSY B

Acknowledgements

Thanks are due to Sam Eakin of Kodak Ltd for giving me permission to use the service call form shown in Figure 7.1.

Part I
Planning for Customer Service

1 The marketing context

What is marketing? How does it apply to the service function? Before reading this chapter, try to answer the test questions given below. The answers are worked through in the chapter itself, and appear as a summary at the end. This question-and-answer format is used throughout the book. It is designed to help you identify immediately the specific subject areas of interest to you.

QUESTIONS

What is the marketing function?

What forces within the control of the marketing manager are traditionally known as the marketing mix?

How can the service manager increase the effectiveness of the marketing mix?

What is a practical technique for researching customer service activities?

What are the main components of a marketing plan for increased customer service effectiveness?

Chapter 1 synopsis
- The meaning of marketing
- The tools for the job
- Looking for improvement
- Practical skills
- Working methods

THE MEANING OF MARKETING

Question What is the marketing function?

Marketing is primarily customer orientation. There are a number of definitions but most say the same thing. They are a function of the literary style or the academic attitude of the author.

The marketing concept has not always dominated business thinking. As recently as the time of the second world war, the underlying motivation of business was – Sell. It was sell with a capital 'S', commonly called the Sales Concept. If one customer did not buy, another was found.

Big business was a battle between the giant companies. It was a slogging match. The lower the price, the more goods that could be sold. Increased turnover gave the manufacturer greater purchasing power. Savings achieved through economies of scale were reflected in lower prices to the consumer. Even greater sales were then achieved – until the product life cycle reached the last stage.

Big business did not want to stop trading when the demand for a product died, so it resolved the problem by increasing the number of products. Business became product oriented. The sales concept had not been dropped – it was reinforced, with a larger number of bigger and better products; and more sales could then be achieved.

With an extensive product range there are problems. Not every product, or product size or product quality is successful. The range is not made up entirely of winners. If it was, business would grow and grow. Getting all the products right is the beginning of marketing. The way to finding the right product at the right price, and having it in the right place, is by going out to the customer. What does the customer want? The marketing concept starts with customer needs.

Around the world there are millions of customers, with countless different needs. But from such a diversity of different customers and markets, it is possible to identify groups of consumers – the buyers – sharing identical needs. Marketers call these groups market segments, and the needs of buyers within a segment are satisfied by the same product or service.

Under the marketing concept, theoretically, all products in a company's range are winners. Each product has specifically been manufactured to satisfy the needs of an identified market segment. When the products sell, the company wins the projected profits. A working definition of marketing has therefore three main aspects:

1 Identifying the needs of buyers and potential buyers in their market segments.
2 Satisfying those needs by selling the appropriate product or service.
3 Making a profit.

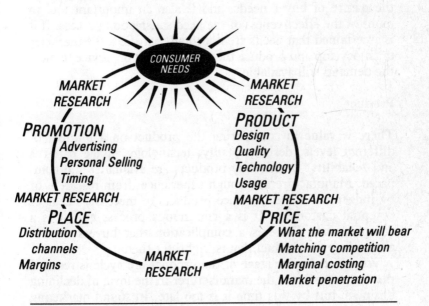

Figure 1.1 The marketing mix – the 4 Ps

Question   **What forces within the control of the marketing manager are traditionally known as the marketing mix?**

In the market place, there are a number of variable forces that the marketing manager controls. It is by manipulating these forces that company objectives are achieved. The variables are PRODUCT, PRICE, PLACE and PROMOTION. Professor Jerome McCarthy called them the four 'P's – the MARKETING MIX – and the name has become universally accepted.

Figure 1.1 shows the marketing mix in diagrammatic form. The starting point is consumer needs. This generic term, covering all needs, from foodstuffs for elephants in zoos, to aviation fuel, is differentiated into smaller and more precise categories known as market segments. Within a segment, all the potential buyers have identical needs.

THE TOOLS FOR THE JOB

Market research is shown in Figure 1.1, between consumer needs and the interacting Ps. Research quantifies and qualifies the nature of buyer needs, and is also an important tool to monitor the effectiveness of the need satisfaction process. If it is ascertained that needs are not totally satisfied, the marketer must develop and produce the right product or service to meet the demand still available.

Product

There is value in considering the product on a number of different levels; design, quality, technology, usage patterns and reliability. In this way products are evaluated and compared. Manufacturers, through experience, from research, or by judgement alone, produce products to meet the needs of potential customers. It is a continuous process and it is a complex one. There is a complication that buyers do not always buy the product that is 'right' for them.

When the decline stage of the product life cycle is reached there are signals for the manufacturer in the form of declining business, but by this time it is too late. In sound marketing practice, regular market research identifies changes in customer needs in time for the manufacturer to adapt and change the product format.

Price

Getting the price right results from knowing what goes on at the place where goods are sold. There are a number of inter-acting factors – whether there is competition, what the competition is charging, or whether the price means status or value for the buyer. For example, it is firmly held by many people that if the price is high the product must be good and, conversely, if the price is low, the product is inferior. In the watch industry, watches with the same movements, but with cosmetically different faces, command widely differing prices, depending on the market segment to which they are offered.

In 1979 Barclays Bank published a report based on 360 interviews with British, French and West German companies. They discovered that there were many instances where agents added 100 or 200 per cent mark-up to their own delivered prices, instead of the traditional 20 to 30 per cent. Having studied the competition and the market place, the agents concluded that they were able to do business at their inflated pricing levels. Incorrect pricing does not mean that business stops, only that profits are being lost or diverted.

Place

Place covers all the distribution paths from the manufacturer to the consumer. A customer buys the product through a number of different channels – by mail order, from shops, from street traders, from vending machines, from depots, or from agents or distributors. Within these channels there are varying discount structures and margins operating for the middlemen involved. The manufacturer or the supplier must decide which distribution channel or channels are appropriate for the product, and more than one channel is often used. An important aspect is whether after-sales service is a factor in the purchase decision. But there must always be flexibility. For example, the second-hand car dealer has occupied the same site for twenty years. He does not command the resources to purchase a second site elsewhere, but there are alternative place options. The dealer can make sure that a show car is displayed at the local carnival, or agricultural show or trade fair. He can make sure that one of his cars is frequently seen at the golf club, or tennis club, or in the car park for Chamber of Commerce functions.

Promotion

Promotion is the 'how' of making the customer buy. Customers do not beat a path to the door of the mousetrap manufacturer unless they are persuaded that they should do so. A large component in promotion is advertising. So is PR. In some cases where there is a relatively small advertising appropriation, PR can be used more effectively than a limited advertising campaign. An example is the House Magazine of a food product manufacturer given free to customers and to retail outlets.

LOOKING FOR IMPROVEMENT

Question How can the service manager increase the effectiveness of the marketing mix?

For many industries, there is an additional variable to those identified in the marketing mix as the four Ps. It is service. The marketing mix should become 'the four Ps and an S' – Product, Place, Promotion, Price and Service.

Service, with few exceptions, is linked to product benefits. Customer expectations of service play an important role in the purchase decision, so it is appropriate, at this point, to define service.

Service is the spectrum of activities designed to enhance customer expectation and enjoyment of product benefits. There are many such activities:

Guarantees
Warranties
Training in product usage
Technical advice
Suggestions for alternative product use

Opportunities to return goods that do not give satisfaction
Repair of defective components
Supply of replacement parts
Follow-up customer contact
Company news letter
Product user clubs and organisations
Monitoring and adapting product performance to meet changing customer needs
Providing dealers and retail outlets with information on current problems and solutions from all customer segments.

The list is not exhaustive. Not all activities apply to every product. Some customers, for example, are confused and daunted by explicit instruction leaflets, like assembly instructions for flat pack furniture units. Others are not. Some demonstrate particular pride in displaying the product ownership badge or emblem. Such an example was at the time the mini motor car was launched by Austin, many years ago, when owners used to flash other owners whom they passed on the road.

By including service in the marketing mix, management has the opportunity to meet marketing objectives specifically oriented to incorporate customer service.

Objective 1 To create maximum customer understanding of product benefits.

Products do not necessarily sell themselves. When product support in respect of maintenance and spare part replacement applies, there is much room for customer doubt and apprehension. Confidence that product support is available must be sold as vigorously as the product itself.

Objective 2 To create maximum customer enjoyment of product benefits.

The professional salesman always sells the product function rather than the product specification. For example, a comb is a strip of plastic or metal designed to arrange the hair in an attractive or functional way. A comb is not a 20cm × 40cm strip of semi-rigid metal of thickness 4mm with 40 serrated teeth of 21mm length and with an overall weight of 56gm.

Objective 3 To generate a percentage of revenue from service support activities.

Service is part of the product as a profit centre. Sub-targets, as examples within this objective are:

● to sell maintenance contracts
● to increase product sales through premium offer concessions
● to gain membership fees from product user clubs
● to generate peripheral and complementary product income.

The customer service operation has to be viewed as a product in itself, and like any product has to be developed, packaged, priced, promoted, communicated and distributed, and so must be marketed in a similar way to the product. First comes research. Next a marketing plan is made, allocating and directing resources of the marketing mix – the four Ps and an S!

PRACTICAL SKILLS

Question **What is a practical technique for researching customer service activities?**

Customer service research starts with an audit of existing practice. The starting point for such research is a planned programme of probing questions. The customer service research audit gathers data for decision making, and it is recorded in appropriate fashion, as shown in Table 1.1, where answers are entered to the following questions:

Customer service research audit

1 What are the customer service objectives?

Objectives should be precise and quantifiable. Compare them with the assessed objectives of competitors.

2 What services are provided?

The following services are listed: repairs, maintenance, customer 'help' telephone number, technical help, alternative product usage, product training, finance, complaint handling, money back guarantee, warranties, other.
    The grid, as illustrated, can be amended to accommodate

Table 1.1
Customer service research audit

Department   Date   Author

	Competitor A	Competitor B	Company
What are the objectives? Published Assumed			
(*Place tick in appropriate square*) What services are provided? Repairs			
Maintenance			
Assembly help phone no.			
Technical help			
Advice on alternative product usage			
Product training			
Finance			
Complaint handling			
Money back guarantee			
Warranties			
Other			
Customer service satisfaction appraisal Ad hoc			
Regular			
Post-delivery			
What additional services do customers want? Last year			
Now			
In future			
How profitable are services? Two years ago			
Last year			
Now			

specific company and industry requirements. Are enough services provided? Would an increase in service to the customer reflect improved business? What support do competitors give?

3   What services do customers want?

How reliable is the knowledge of customer needs? What awareness is there by the customers of the services already provided? Are the services provided, perceived by the customers as important? What influence does service support have on the customer's purchase decision?

4   How profitable are the services?

Service must not be free. It is a commodity for sale. How effectively are the services priced? Where can margins be increased? What incentives operate to generate improved effectiveness from service personnel?

5   What is the stage of the service life cycle?

For some services the cycle is short. An example is customer education. With domestic appliances, computer hardware, and security control systems there are significant service requirements during the customer learning process. With motor cars there is much activity in the early stages of ownership. This coincides with the period of the warranty where the customer is not charged realistic prices, if any, to resolve product defects.

WORKING METHODS

Question   **What are the main components of a marketing plan for increased customer service effectiveness?**

A marketing plan in the format of working checklists is implemented with relative ease. There are four main areas of customer service that a marketing plan must cover: customer education, staff education, customer complaint administration, and costing levels. A checklist is provided for each. They probe the levels of customer service that determine the marketing success or failure of the customer service activity.

Customer education

Customer education checklist

Place tick in appropriate box YES NO

● Are product usage/assembly instructions clearly and precisely given? ☐ ☐

● Is customer understanding of instructions monitored regularly? ☐ ☐

● Is customer training freely available? ☐ ☐

● Do potential customers know the extent of service back-up available? ☐ ☐

● Do PR and media activities inform customers of all product benefits? ☐ ☐

● Do the public at large know of the company and its products? ☐ ☐

● Do the public think that the company cares? ☐ ☐

If the answer to each question is Yes, OK. If No, do something about it.

Staff education

Staff education checklist

Place tick in appropriate box YES NO

● Is there specific staff training in telephone techniques? ☐ ☐

● Is there an induction training programme for new employees? ☐ ☐

● Are staff trained for face-to-face meetings with customers and the public? ☐ ☐

Place tick in appropriate box   YES   NO

- Do customer needs take priority over in-
house company activities?   ☐   ☐

- Is management action taken when employee
irritation with customers is identified?   ☐   ☐

- Is there specific staff training in respect of
PR – adverse and favourable – that is generated
by employee conduct?   ☐   ☐

- Do the staff like the customers?   ☐   ☐

- Do the staff know about customer levels of
expectation?   ☐   ☐

- Are there specific incentives to motivate
staff?   ☐   ☐

- Do staff have job satisfaction?   ☐   ☐

If the answer to each question is Yes, OK. If No, do something about it.

Customer complaints administration

Customer complaints checklist

Place tick in appropriate box   YES   NO

- Is there a house policy regarding customer
complaints?   ☐   ☐

- Is there a standardised complaint response
procedure?   ☐   ☐

- Are complaints procedure documents used
for customer complaint calls?   ☐   ☐

- Are complaints recorded?   ☐   ☐

- Are complaints analysed regularly for management action?   ☐   ☐

Place tick in appropriate box   YES   NO

- Is the cost of the complaint response procedure known? ☐ ☐
- Have the problems of complaint categories over six months old been resolved? ☐ ☐
- Has sub-contract liability for customer complaints been apportioned? ☐ ☐
- Are staff sympathetic towards customer complaint problems? ☐ ☐
- Have staff been trained to deal with angry customers? ☐ ☐

If the answer to each question is Yes, OK. If No, do something about it.

Costing levels

Costing levels checklist

Place tick in appropriate box   YES   NO

- Are service activities a profit centre? ☐ ☐
- If service activities are a cost centre, could they be changed now to a profit centre? ☐ ☐
- Have margins been increased in the last six months? ☐ ☐
- Would there be customer acceptance if all service charges were uplifted by 10, 20, 30 or 40 per cent now? ☐ ☐
- What are the margins taken by competitors? ☐ ☐
- Is the cost of every single service activity known? ☐ ☐
- Is there an incentive scheme to motivate service personnel? ☐ ☐

If the answer to each question is Yes, OK. If No, do something about it.

SUMMARY

Question   **What is the marketing function?**

Answer   Marketing has three main aspects, (*1*) identifying the needs of buyers and potential buyers in their market segments, (*2*) satisfying those needs by selling the appropriate product or service, and (*3*) making a profit.

Question   **What forces within the control of the marketing manager are traditionally known as the marketing mix?**

Answer   The traditional marketing mix comprises the four Ps – Product, Place, Price and Promotion.

Question   **How can the service manager increase the effectiveness of the marketing mix?**

Answer   By upgrading the marketing mix to 'four Ps and an S' – Product, Price, Place, Promotion and Service – management secures greatest control of the variables that they direct in the market place.

Question   **What is a practical technique for researching customer service activities?**

Answer   Customer service activities are researched effectively with a customer service research audit.

Question   **What are the main components of a marketing plan for increased customer service effectiveness?**

Answer   The main components of customer service marketing are (*1*) customer education, (*2*) employee education, (*3*) customer complaint administration, and (*4*) costing levels.

2 Customer expectations of service

Before reading this chapter, try to answer the test questions given below. The answers will emerge in the chapter itself and appear in a summary at the end.

QUESTIONS

How constant are customer expectations of service?

What factors influence customer expectations of service?

How does a service manager evaluate the standard of employee response to customer enquiries?

What staff training can improve a customer's low expectation of service?

Chapter 2 synopsis

- The rise and fall of expectations
- Attracting and deterring customers
- Researching the problem
- Practical help

THE RISE AND FALL OF EXPECTATIONS

Question How constant are customer expectations of service?

Customer expectations are attitudes held by customers towards a company. They relate to the product, to the service given, and to the professionalism of customer contact. When a company is approached for the first time, expectations can be high. Without adverse experience, there is, theoretically, no reason for the expectation of the response to be anything other than professional and competent.

But large companies and organisations offering service to the public do not operate in a vacuum. Even where an individual has not had personal contact before, often he or she is aware of the experience of others. The needs of customers requiring service are specific. They need help, of one kind or another; they require information, or their equipment is malfunctioning, or they are running out of supplies.

There is always a degree of urgency, perhaps emergency, in the call for service. Tensions are created that build up with every moment of delay before the customer problem is resolved. Customers or potential customers calling for service, are, therefore, seldom unprejudiced. There is influence, for good or ill, by the way the company has handled previous requests for service. So when a customer has had experience of dealing with a company, expectations are directly coloured by the efficiency and smoothness of the earlier contact.

An experiment was conducted by the author, as a training resource for courses on customer relations. Enquiries, seeking information, were made by telephone to ten companies. The conversations were recorded on audio tape. The companies are British Airways, British Rail, Alpine Double Glazing, Crittall Windows, Thermobreak, Bristol Street Motors, Oxford Motors, Quick Fit Euro, Electricity Board and Anglian Water Board.

Some of the companies responded well, others badly. In the classroom, usually all, or nearly all, the names of the companies were known to the participants.

In the exercise, the taped calls are played to the class. Before each call the name of the company is given, and also the nature

Table 2.1
Level of expectation grid

Call	Reliability	Confidence	Helpfulness	Efficiency	Personal Interest	Your rating of Level of Expectation	Your rating of L. of E. for next call
1							
2							
3							
4							
5							
6							
7							
8							
9							
10							

Place tick in appropriate square every time one of the listed qualities in the service is perceived.
Rate your level of expectation on a scale of 0 – 10, with zero as the lowest expectation.

of the enquiry that the class are about to hear being made. Participants are asked to rate, on a scale of 0 to 10, the expectation of service that will be provided. If an extremely bad response is expected the rating is 0. If superlative service is expected the rating is 10.

Class participants are provided with a grid, to help them to monitor the calls of the exercise. This grid is illustrated in Table 2.1. In the appropriate columns, participants enter their level of expectation before hearing a call. In the adjacent column participants are asked to rate the same company again, after the call has been played to them. What quality of response do they now expect from the company, in the light of what they have just heard?

In the limited context of training courses run by one lecturer, the conclusions are overwhelmingly significant. The level of expectation never stays the same. The pattern of movement however, is invariably uniform. Every time the exercise is used, the level of expectation of companies that the class upgrades in the light of hearing the tapes rises by an average of one point. Companies that are downgraded drop by an average of three points. Is the exercise a microcosm of all customer expectations of service? How do customers rate your company on a scale of 10?

ATTRACTING AND DETERRING CUSTOMERS

Question   **What factors influence customer expectations of service?**

The response given by a company to the public, or to an existing customer is evaluated on a number of levels:

Efficiency. Is the caller given precisely the information or related action that is sought? If the response is business-like, and provided without undue delay, then the response is efficient.

Confidence. People making an enquiry, or a request, invest authority in the person to whom they are speaking. Provided that the person giving the response has confidence, that authority is reinforced. Even if the information given is incorrect it is often accepted if the manner of the person does not belie the validity. When confidence is lacking, whether action is being taken or information being provided, the presentation is undermined. Effectiveness is diminished.

Helpfulness. Helpfulness is a bonus. Helpfulness is when a caller is assisted in his or her enquiry, by suggestions and possibly relevant information and action that are greater, or in more detail than the particular response or action sought.

Personal interest. When personal interest is shown in answering a customer enquiry, the relationship is changed. Initially, it is them and us. With personal interest it changes to a one-to-one caring relationship. Caring relationships are pleasing. They are remembered favourably.

Reliability. The image of reliability is much sought after by companies. It means that the customer can depend on performance and response. He or she knows that a reliable company fulfils its commitments.

The above are intrinsic factors. They influence the response of the company employee to the customer and to the public. Intrinsic factors are susceptible to training. They can be improved by training when performance does not reach set standards.

Additionally, external factors exist. These are outside the response given by the employee.

Media influence. Media support for the company and its products exerts a positive influence on expectations.

Hearsay. The experience of others contributes to customer expectations. Adverse experiences are related by one person to another much more frequently than positive experiences.

In the classroom exercise described above participants evaluate the factors listed, when they listen to the recorded tapes. Column headings in the grid (Table 2.1) guide the judgements that are made. Participants put a tick in an appropriate column every time they identify a particular factor. Absence of column ticks exposes reasons for low ratings. In the service call, enquiries are made to the companies and recorded for the exercise; the information required is not extensive. An example is a flight timetable enquiry London – Dusseldorf – Milan – London. The other calls are of a similar nature. The length of time taken by companies in giving their responses varies considerably.

The longest call lasts eleven minutes. The length is primarily due to the long silences which occur. The silences in the call, listened to by tutor and class together, are more eloquent than any words the tutor can provide. Keeping the customer hanging on and on is a cardinal sin. But it is not the only sin. Others are lack of interest, sloppiness, impatience, aggression and incompetence.

RESEARCHING THE PROBLEM

Question   How does a service manager evaluate the standard of employee response to customer enquiries?

Perhaps of greatest concern to a manager is that area of business contact from which there is no immediate customer response. When a motor car is serviced, or a householder's carpet cleaned, the customer is likely to protest if the quality of the service supplied is poor. When a quotation stage precedes service action, the manager is not often in a position to know if the preliminary standards are low. Potential customers who are aggrieved, or dissatisfied, or simply unimpressed, are likely to go elsewhere.

A fall in the existing levels of business is usually the first signal to a manager that something is wrong. If business does not drop off, there is perhaps no signal, but there can still be great room for improvement. Badly managed customer enquiries prevent substantial increases in new or repeat business.

Controlled feedback is necessary on staff performance. Random observation plays a part, but employee performance is known to improve under management scrutiny. The process of monitoring staff performance can also be dealt with by an independent third party contact, or a self-administered questionnaire response by employees.

Table 2.2

Third party contact grid

	Efficiency	Confidence	Helpfulness	Personal interest	Reliability	Rudeness	Delay before responding	Delay during response	Incompetence Much | Little	Indifference Much | Little
Call A am Lunchtime pm										
Call B am Lunchtime pm										
Call C am Lunchtime pm										
Call D am Lunchtime pm										
Call E am Lunchtime pm										
Call F am Lunchtime pm										
Call G am Lunchtime pm										

Third party contact

Enquiries are made by an independent person or persons and the responses given evaluated. It is helpful to use a grid, of appropriate format as illustrated in Table 2.2. The responses are recorded for enquiries made at pre-set times. The minimum number of contacts should be three, comprising morning, lunch time and late afternoon. Lunch time is particularly susceptible to poor response levels unless management makes a specific effort to maintain a standard.

Analysis of the data collected demonstrates the positive and the negative qualities in employee performance. The positive qualities are:

Efficiency
Confidence
Helpfulness
Personal interest
Reliability

The negative qualities are:

Rudeness
Delay before response
Delay during response
Incompetence
Indifference

With a person working for a company that is generally efficient, it is not expected that an entry appears in every column for particular calls. Even with very good, experienced people, there are delays and periods of silence during a call. Delays are sometimes unavoidable, but the irritation and bad feeling engendered by such delays can be neutralised by helpfulness and efficiency. If the customer is advised continuously of delay problems, and approached sympathetically, the outcome can be positive.

Self-administered questionnaire

In the majority of cases where performance is poor, the staff are not aware of the damage they do to their company. If asked a direct question on the value of good PR to their company, they understand that it is helpful. This understanding does not translate directly into their answering every customer enquiry efficiently and without delay. Employees involved in customer contact, such as providing information, or telling the public how to follow directions, perceive their roles from their own personal frame of reference. Work consists of answering questions about products or services, sitting or standing at a particular place. It means being present in the company from 9.00 am to 5.00 pm five or six days a week. It is not often seen in the wider context of being part of a relationship, albeit transient, with customers and members of the public.

The manager's task is to motivate his or her team to identify with the needs of the public. When this is achieved, the standard of response to enquiries from customers and from the public can be very high. The self-administered questionnaire is a useful tool to help meet that purpose by exposing weaknesses. It identifies how employees see their role, and their effectiveness. The questionnaire is best used in conjunction with the third party contact. If weaknesses are identified by third party contact, the questionnaire reveals whether staff are aware of the nature of their performance. The questionnaire is shown in Figure 2.1.

PRACTICAL HELP

Question **What staff training can improve a customer's low expectation of service?**

The different aspects of staff performance fall, broadly speaking, into two categories.

Category 1	*Category 2*
Efficiency	Helpfulness
Reliability	Personal interest
Prompt reaction	Caring
Courtesy	Confidence
Professional manner	Indifference
Confidence	Rudeness

Category 1 relates to the structure of employee activities. The more precise the sequence of actions and responses that the

Place tick in appropriate column	nil	little	av.	much	v.much
1 What confidence do I show to callers?					
2 What efficiency do I demonstrate?					
3 What reliability do I offer?					
4 What degree of caring do I give?					
5 What personal interest do I show?					
6 What length of time, on average, are callers kept waiting before I answer?					
7 What delays occur during calls?					
8 What is the proportion of callers with whom I get angry?					
9 What is the proportion of callers who get angry with me?					
10 What is the proportion of callers who are rude to me?					
11 What is the proportion of callers who are difficult customers?					
12 What is the proportion of callers who are unreasonable?					
13 What improvements could be made in company procedure for dealing with customer enquiries?					
14 What contribution does my work make to establishing good PR?					

Figure 2.1   Self-administered questionnaire

employee is asked to make, the greater are the levels of performance. Category 2 relates to the individual personal contributions that are complementary and supportive to category 1.

The factor of confidence is placed in both groups. It can be manufactured from acquired competence and skills. It is also an innate component of the personality make-up of some fortunate individuals.

Training has to be geared to the two categories. The objective of the training to meet the needs of category 1 is to provide a framework. It is a pattern of response that an employee learns. When that pattern is used, the responses to customer enquiries are competent and efficient.

The objective of training for category 2 is different. It is to motivate participants in the training situation to produce, from within themselves, personal qualities that enhance the acquired skills learned under category 1 training.

Category 1 training

The complexity of the training pattern varies with different industries. A timetable enquiry made to the office of a national bus service demands precise factual information: that is all. A request for service from the owner of a broken washing machine demands remedial action. The structure of the call response is the same for both types of enquiries, but the response to the latter caller is expanded to meet wider needs.

Step 1. Smile when you speak to the caller. Whether face-to-face, or from the other end of a telephone, a friendly courteous manner communicates itself. Smiling at the end of the day is harder than smiling first thing in the morning. With practice, smiling becomes a habit. The results are rewarding.

Step 2. Identify your department. On the telephone it is important to say who you are. 'Hello' is friendly, but is neither productive nor efficient. When the call is through a switchboard, giving the name of the department is appropriate. If the call is directly from outside, the company name is given first. If there are many companies on the same number, the number is given. The actual name of the person answering the call is only sometimes applicable. It is not applicable when someone is asking for the price of theatre seats, or needing the day's weather forecast.

The name of the person answering should be given when it is necessary for the caller to expect action arising from the call just made. A name is a point of contact in what may appear to the caller as a vast anonymous organisation.

Step 3. Establish the caller's needs. Find out by questioning precisely what the needs are. Sometimes they are volunteered by the caller. Not everyone is articulate; many people have difficulty in expressing themselves. The questions to the caller who needs help should first pinpoint the general area of help needed. The final questions localise the problem for the caller.

Callers' needs should be written on a pad. Many companies print special forms; others who have computer systems provide Visual Display Units. Records should always have the caller's name, telephone number and other details – equipment specification/model number, nature of problem, date and time, name of person dealing with the problem, nature of the solution, confirmation that matter is closed.

Step 4. Provide the information or help required. Telling the customer what you're doing, whilst you are doing it, breaks up silence. If it is necessary for you to put the telephone down or leave the counter for a moment, say so. When the call is going to mean a visit from a service engineer, there is usually no need for further communication between you and the caller. Make sure, always, that the customer has a clear, realistic understanding of when the visit is scheduled to take place and the company terms for such a call.

Step 5. Make sure that the customer or member of the public concludes the enquiry with the feeling that the company cares. Enquirers after information are thanked for their interest. Callers seeking service engineer attention, or despatch of replacement parts, must perceive the commitment of the company to their needs. It is especially for 'action' calls that leaving a name with the caller, as described in step 2, is important.

There are two additional inter-related stages.

Additional step A. Dealing with complaints. This step is not always applicable. The initial part is to listen. The full details of the complaint must be known. Never argue. Handling a complaint requires diplomacy. This step normally falls between step 3 and step 4.

Additional step B. Dealing with angry customers. Usually angry customers have a complaint and ultimately are dealt with as in step A. Angry customers, however, do not always slot easily into the standard response format. The anger is communicated strongly the moment contact with a company employee is achieved. The problems of angry customers are dealt with in depth in Chapter Ten. The important rules to remember are listen, be sympathetic, be diplomatic, and never argue. The prime emphasis is on the listening. The customer who is not materially interrupted defuses his or her own anger to the point where appropriate action can be set in motion, in accordance with normal customer response procedures.

Category 2 training

The different objective to that of category 1 calls for a different training technique. Motivation of employees to produce personal qualities has to be generated from within themselves. The training is most effectively achieved in a classroom situation.

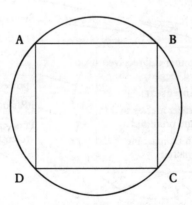

Figure 2.2 Customer needs and company responses

The class is divided into syndicates of about three persons. Each syndicate is provided with a diagram, as per Figure 2.2, printed on an A4 size sheet of paper. The circle represents overall customer needs. Square ABCD represents company responses capable of satisfying those needs. The task for the participants to carry out is as follows:

1 In the customer needs circle, write a specific customer enquiry detailing the major requirements.

2 In the square ABCD, write the actions comprising the basic company response necessary to satisfy the needs described above.

3 Fill up the space within the circle, not taken up by square ABCD, with as many segments as possible. Each segment represents an enhancing contribution that improves the quality of the response to the customer. The nature of each contribution is written within the segment. Examples of contributions are the name of the person dealing with the enquiry, expressions of sympathy, advice, encouragement, confidence boosting stories of company and product achievements.

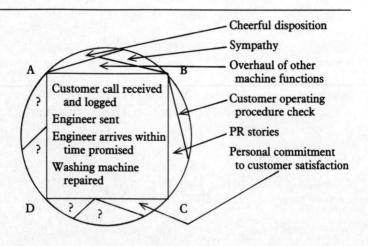

Figure 2.3 Response to a call for a washing machine repair

The exercise is made competitive between the syndicates. Winners are those who produce the greatest number of valid contribution segments. Maximum effectiveness is achieved from this training resource by class discussion of the results, followed by an individual commitment extracted from participants that they practise the contributions they have identified and developed.

An example is given of the exercise devised for staff employed by manufacturers of domestic home appliances. Figure 2.3 illustrates the response to a service call for a broken washing machine.

SUMMARY

Question How constant are customer expectations of service?

Answer   Customer expectations of service are not constant at all. They are extremely volatile.

Question   What factors influence customer expectations of service?

Answer   Customer expectations are influenced by the professionalism and confidence of the person dealing with the enquiry, by media influence and by hearsay.

Question   How does a service manager evaluate the standard of employee response to customer enquiries?

Answer   There are three options available to a manager to evaluate standards of employee response. They are (*1*) personal observation, (*2*) third party contact and (*3*) self-administered questionnaire.

Question   What staff training can improve a customer's low expectation of service?

Answer   There are two training activities to lift low expectations of customer service, (1) instituting standard response procedures, and (2) a classroom training exercise to develop personal qualities that enhance the standard of response given.

3 Staff management and training

Before reading this chapter, try to answer the test questions given below. The answers will emerge in the chapter itself and appear in a summary at the end.

QUESTIONS

What are the most important functions of a service manager?

What is the first task a newly appointed manager of a customer service department carries out?

How is the manager able to plan future performance of the customer service department?

How are staff helped to deal with customer problems in the most effective way?

How is a high standard of customer service developed and maintained?

What is a good way to motivate customer service department staff?

What guidelines are helpful to a training programme?

Chapter 3 synopsis

- Management scope
- The way to manage
- Getting the future right
- Helping staff to help
- Keeping up standards
- Motivating to win
- The best way to train

MANAGEMENT SCOPE

Question **What are the most important functions of a service manager?**

Irrespective of the size of a service department, certain functions are common to all. They are organising, controlling, motivating and training.

Organising

There are good and bad ways of dealing with customers and their needs. Left to themselves, staff responses range between these two extremes. As the pressures of fatigue and tedium increase, staff response deteriorates. The manager's task is to keep the standard of response and reaction above an acceptable minimum level.

Staff need a model on which to base their behaviour. Organising means designing and planning a standardised pattern of behaviour to meet appropriate situations. There are many examples – how to speak to the customer who telephones for information, how to greet a customer waiting in the depot or how to pacify an angry owner of malfunctioning equipment.

Sometimes company procedures evolve with time. The momentum of habit stifles initiative and change. Another task of the manager is periodically to evaluate the way things are done now. Do changing customer needs demand different ways of meeting them?

Controlling

Controlling is day-to-day management, and includes over-seeing, timekeeping, standards of dress, standards of discipline, eating patterns and grievance handling. It consists of arranging work schedules, holiday rotas and absentee substitution with no precise demarcation for each function. Sometimes the functions are shared with a Personnel Department or officer. Recruitment particularly is an aspect that Personnel undertake, although for greatest success the job specification should be written by the service manager.

Motivating

When the pattern of work is easily quantifiable, as in production and in sales, the problems of motivation are often simplified. Financial incentives spur staff to meeting and beating targets. These solutions do not necessarily apply to every service function, as the following questions illustrate. How are information providing or complaint handling activities quantified? What targets can be set for the employee whose work is to direct the public in one or another direction?

An important weapon in the armoury of motivation for the customer service manager is praise. But praise cannot be used in isolation. The working environment has to be structured so that praise is meaningful. Through training, the remaining prime function, the manager instills an awareness in the staff of the contribution that each makes to company progress. Each member of staff must understand how their individual performance generates good or bad PR. It is easy for a manager to give an occasional pep talk, but much more difficult to make the pep talk stick. One method is for the staff to write their own code of practice, and then adopt it.

Training

Training is the process of giving others skills. It is itself a skill. There are a number of techniques, one of the most important of which is embodied in the concept 'learning is doing'. Training effectiveness is never directly proportional to the number of words spoken by the person carrying out the training.

The first part of a manager's training function is to identify training needs, and then the training programme can be planned. The 'drip-feed' schedule is more effective than the one-off training session, but there are advantages and disadvantages to each programme. With both programmes it is best that participants are taken away from their working environment, although this is sometimes difficult for short period 'drip-feed' training. Ideally they should be away, because the training class needs to be insulated from day-to-day demands on attention and time during the training period.

The optimum size of a training group is between nine and fifteen. It is not always possible to release this number of staff together. But the results of training are most effective when there is group interaction. A class of nine to fifteen trainees divides easily into three or four syndicates, and it is from the syndicate exercises set by the trainer that most learning is achieved. The members of the group work out problems and are helped to reach conclusions for themselves.

When there are many more staff to be trained it is tempting from a cost and convenience point of view to make the classes larger, and, although the manager who is good at training can control larger numbers, the learning effectiveness is diluted because there is less time available for each participant to make an individual contribution. Alternatively some participants are unable to make any contribution individually at all. When this situation occurs, no glaring signals of lost learning achievement are given, especially when the administration of the training is smooth and efficient, but academic research on training effectiveness concludes positively that the more successful results derive from small rather than large classes.

The most successful results of all, measured by mastery of specific skills, and by retention of learned information, derive from the 'drip-feed' process. A one-day training session in each of three consecutive months obtains better results than one three-day training session.

THE WAY TO MANAGE

Managing is a skill that is made up of a lot of other skills embodied in the functions described above. Managers manage best if their activities are planned and structured. A comprehensive set of rules governing that planning and structuring simplifies the problem of good management. The following pages develop such a set of rules – *The Golden Rules of Managing the Customer Service Function*. Questions are asked about customer service activities. From the answers the rules are formulated.

Question **What is the first task a newly appointed manager of a customer service department carries out?**

A manager must know the what, and the how, and the where, of his job. What is expected of him or her? What must the department achieve? What resources of finance, personnel, equipment, material, transport and accommodation are available? What are the line responsibilities within the management hierarchy? How is performance measured? Where are the geographical boundaries of responsibility?

A convenient format for the audit is a grid, as in Figure 3.1, showing typical questions to be asked to generate the required information. For each company the manager must write his own questions.

1 What are the relevant company objectives?

The service department operates in the context of overall company activities. There is little value in organising a team of fifty service engineers if sales achieve only a few installations. How is the service department to interface with other functions of corporate activity?

2 List all service function activities. Evaluate observed performance on a five point scale: 1 – very bad, 2 – bad, 3 – mediocre, 4 – good, 5 – very good.

3 What staff complement is necessary to meet performance objectives? Projected? Actual?

When taking over control of a department, especially if promoted from within, it is essential to view the total operation objectively. Are staffing levels inflated, adequate or

Department

Date

What are company objectives?
What are departmental objectives?

	Bad				Good
Performance of service functions	1	2	3	4	5
A					
B					
C					
D					
Staff complement for service functions					
Projected					
Actual					
Cost savings for functions					
A					
B					
C					
D					
Market pricing levels for functions					
A					
B					
C					
D					
Date of last training programme					
Staff evaluation of own performance	1	2	3	4	5
E					
F					
G					
H					
Additional equipment/resources etc. required					

Figure 3.1   Departmental activity audit grid

inadequate? Is the calibre of the staff adequate for the demands upon them to be met?

4   If the department is a cost centre, what savings can be achieved?

Each cost item is evaluated. Are procedural or performance changes possible in order to reduce costs? Is it feasible to change the department to a profit centre? Monitoring costs on a regular basis is important.

5   If the department is a profit centre, which items are below market pricing levels?

Which margins can be increased now? By how much? Are there additional services that can be sold? What percentage of customer base gives repeat business? Getting the financial aspect right is a major component of good management.

6   When was the last training programme carried out?

What did the training cover? How was it validated? How often is training repeated? What induction courses are mounted for new staff? What are current training needs? What training resources exist? Answering these questions gives a reliable picture of the training perspective.

7   How do staff rate their own performance?

Care must be taken that answers are not distorted because the questions are perceived as threats. The answers can be compared with the opinions of customers and independent third parties, on the receiving end of the service function.

8   What equipment, resources, information, do the staff not have that they would like to have?

It is of value to know what the staff want to have. Management must evaluate whether supplying that need is cost effective and productive.

The departmental activity audit provides a picture of where the customer service function is. The manager is then able to make decisions as to where he or she wants it to go. So the first Golden Rule is formulated.

Golden Rule no 1 Design and Carry out a Customer Service Department Audit

GETTING THE FUTURE RIGHT

Question How is the manager able to plan future performance of the customer service department?

When objectives are precise they translate into targets. The targets can be in money terms, in production terms, in standards of behaviour and performance – or the targets can relate to any specific customer service activities not falling under the headings given. It is essential to have such targets; then the manager has a yardstick to measure progress. The second Golden Rule is formulated.

Golden Rule no 2 Set Customer Service Department Objectives

HELPING STAFF TO HELP

Question How are staff helped to deal with customer problems in the most effective way?

Mrs Brown buys a hairdryer from a department store. It blows cold air but not hot air, so Mrs Brown telephones, not the department store, but the manufacturer. She wants to ask what the manufacturer is going to do about it. The call is put through first to production, and then to the customer liaison department. There are a variety of responses that the employee taking the call can give, ranging from 'Don't know' to precise informed instructions.

The problem has to be thought through in advance. Standardised response procedure starts when Mrs Brown speaks to the switchboard. All service-related calls must be routed to a particular person or persons nominated to deal with them. A specific routine, appropriate to all the customer problems that are met, has to be planned in advance. It is as well to make a contingency plan to deal with the situation that has not yet been allowed for.

The plan is then communicated to everyone concerned with incoming service calls or complaints. The plan must be printed. The format is such that new or temporary staff need only ask set questions in the order that is printed. Customer replies, information and requirements are entered as they are received onto the printed customer response form, as shown in Figure 3.2.

With such a standardised response procedure, initiative is not necessary. Efficiency and professionalism take over. This concept reflects the next Golden Rule.

Golden Rule no 3 Devise and Introduce Standard Response Procedures for dealing with specific customer problems

KEEPING UP STANDARDS

Question How is a high standard of customer service developed and maintained?

Standardised response procedures to deal with customer problems, as prescribed by Golden Rule no 3 are very important. But they are not the whole story. Service department staff have to initiate many activities that are not customer problem related. A main aim of every customer service department is to help create satisfied customers. This means preventing customers having problems. Talking to customers, giving them information, caring, helping, being reliable. All these are aspects of good customer relations. They do not necessarily happen spontaneously.

Training makes them happen – if the training is designed and planned to meet specific company needs. Like all skills, training is not a magic process that works every time because it has been practised. Feedback is necessary after the training session to identify how well it has been absorbed, and then

To: From:

Enquiry taken by: date:

Customer need:

Action promised:

Action taken:

_____

Customer name:

Company address:

Tel. no.:

Additional information:

_____

Figure 3.2   Printed standard customer response form

follows the acid test. Performance and behaviour of the participants should demonstrate improvement and achievement.

A regular training programme must build in a flexibility to adapt, if the results projected do not materialise. A simple training needs audit grid, as illustrated in Figure 3.3, is helpful in identifying current training needs. The manager enters the name of each member of staff, in the spaces provided. Against each name in turn a cross is inserted where training is needed, in each of the columns across the page. The audit is used two, three or four times a year, as appropriate to the company and circumstances. Golden Rule no 4 is now indicated.

Golden Rule no 4 Initiate Regular Training Programmes to satisfy identified training needs

MOTIVATING TO WIN

Question **What is a good way to motivate customer service department staff?**

Motivation takes various forms. It can be a financial bonus, a competition prize, or a pep talk. Motivation can come from within, or from the example and success of colleagues. One excellent form of motivation is praise and recognition. There are few people who do not like to be patted on the back; praise means that effort has not passed unnoticed.

Managers are often quick to single out mistakes and poor performance, but good performance and efforts made by staff genuinely trying hard, must also be noticed and praised, even if they are not successful. 'John, I thought you handled that customer particularly well. You struck just the right balance of authority and contrition. Well done.' 'Margaret, you sorted those leaflets for the customer very professionally. I hope she is as impressed as I am.' Praise is the most effective when it is given in front of others. Because of its importance, the process of praising constitutes the fifth Golden Rule.

Golden Rule no 5 Seek out Opportunities to Praise Staff for actions they have performed well

Staff	Speaking on telephone	Face to face	Communi-cating	Profession-alism	Personal appearance	Time-keeping	Loyalty

Place cross where training is needed. Carry out audit at three-monthly intervals.

Figure 3.3   Training needs audit

THE BEST WAY TO TRAIN

Question **What guidelines are helpful to a training programme?**

A good trainer plans his/her training programme meticulously, and rehearses thoroughly before any training session. An experienced lecturer can go into the classroom without preparation, and cope on an *ad hoc* basis, but the results are not as good as when there is prior preparation.

A useful format for training seminars is as follows:

● Restrict class sizes to about fifteen participants. Larger sizes become unwieldy, and learning achievement diminishes.

● The trainer gives an initial short introductory lecture. Visual aids in the form of overhead projector slides, flip charts, posters or models are invaluable. Handouts are useful too, if they take away the need for the trainees to make notes whilst the lecturer is talking. If handouts are not provided, the lecturer should allow time for salient facts to be copied. On no account, however, should the session turn into a dictation period.

● Exercises are set for the participants to work through. For example, prepare a list of do's and don'ts for dealing with an angry customer. The class is divided into small groups or syndicates, and when each syndicate has reached a conclusion the class reassembles, and each syndicate presents its findings. From all the material presented an agreed conclusion is then drawn.

● A commitment is obtained from each participant to behave or perform in a manner decided by the class as appropriate. A personal commitment to do something is a strong motivating force, and the person who makes such a commitment is likely to uphold it, at least for a short time. A word of caution, however, is appropriate. The commitment should be verbal and diplomatically handled. A written commitment can carry the interpretation of an infringement of individual rights, even though the peer group may have decided on the format and extent of the commitment.

There is one fundamental principle of training practice. It is that trainees should *do* rather than *be told*. If a participant in a training session works something out, he or she remembers it far more effectively than if he or she is merely told that it is so.

The appendix at the end of this chapter (pages 47–64) shows how an appropriate training programme can be developed.

SUMMARY

Question   **What are the most important functions of a service manager?**

Answer   The most important functions of a service manager are (*1*) organising (*2*) controlling (*3*) motivating and (*4*) training.

Question   **What is the first task a newly appointed manager of a customer service department carries out?**

Answer   A newly appointed manager's first task is to design and carry out a department activity audit.

Question   **How is the manager able to plan future performance of the customer service department?**

Answer   The manager sets customer service department objectives.

Question   **How are staff helped to deal with customer problems in the most effective way?**

Answer   Standardised customer response procedures are devised to help staff cope with every customer problem.

Question   **How is a high standard of customer service developed and maintained?**

Answer Regular training is the most effective means of providing first class customer service.

Question **What is a good way to motivate customer service department staff?**

Answer Praise staff whenever they act in a commendable way.

Question **What guidelines are helpful to a training programme?**

Answer For training to be successful, ensure that (*1*) the class contains no more than fifteen participants, (*2*) training style is interactive, and (*3*) participants are supplied with handouts summarising material studied.

APPENDIX TO CHAPTER 3

Training task

Develop a detailed training programme for the following exercise:

Satellite Communications Ltd are manufacturers of high tech communication equipment. Product applications are in rocketry and interplanetary travel.

The company is exhibiting for two weeks at an important industry trade fair in the United Kingdom. Through ill health, a marriage, and a combination of circumstances, only one technical sales engineer is available each day to man the stand, and the company is extremely busy. Although a recruitment programme has been mounted, the company is short staffed.

Management decides that two other persons must join the engineer on the stand each day. A rota of ten persons has been drawn up to share the task, taken from the engineering services department, accounts department, and the general office. As far as possible, they have been selected for qualities of confidence and ability.

You are the manager of the engineering services department. The managing director has sent you a memo saying that, because of the indisposition of the marketing manager, would you please organise the training of all the staff attending the exhibition. A copy of your training programme is requested, to file for future exhibitions.

What do you do?

Training exercise model answer

The training programme is planned. First it is named. The programme is entitled: Manning the Satellite Communication Exhibition stand, a one day training seminar.

The planning steps are:

(a) Set objectives for programme

The objectives are going to reflect everything that participants at the exhibition will try to achieve, how they set about it, and what they need to know.

Appropriate objectives are formulated, so that by the end of the seminar, participants must:

- be familiar with the exhibition venue, timetable, and organisers' statutory requirements
- have developed and practised a procedure for greeting visitors to the stand
- have learned specification details of product range to an acceptable minimum level
- understand the relevance of an employee's confident, cheerful, professional manner to good PR.

Once the objectives are set, it is possible to identify the resources that are needed. Specialist instructors, if required, must be booked. A venue has also to be booked and appropriate materials ordered. The precise sequence of events that follow the setting of objectives is not significant. It is best to book the venue as early as possible, unless company facilities are such that there are no problems. The next step is:

(b) Arrange venue

Book the training room for the period required. Itemise the equipment and resources needed:

Tables with ten chairs arranged in U-shape
Lecturer's table and chair at opening of U but with space between, so as to allow lecturer to walk into the U area
Overhead slide projector
Low table to support slide projector
Screen
Video recorder/camera, monitor
Table to support monitor
Paper
Nameplate stands
Folders for handout notes
Pens
Water beakers and glasses
Flip chart
Demonstration equipment
Surplus chairs and table to accommodate casual visitors
Waste paper baskets.

This last item, waste paper baskets, is extremely useful. Surplus paper in the form of excess printed handouts, or wrappings, is usually a problem. The lecturer's table must never become cluttered or it looks unprofessional. It can impede the smooth flow of the programme if notes or overhead slides are buried beneath a mound of paper.

Figure 3A.1 illustrates a convenient classroom layout.

It is useful to give participants on a training programme as much advance warning as possible, so that they can make suitable arrangements in regard to their absence from normal duties. Ideally, an outline programme of the training seminar is given too.

When the seminar programme is structured for participants in advance, they have an opportunity to think about the subject. With experience, trainers can write a programme giving recise times of sessions, and then develop sessional material to fit within the allocated time.

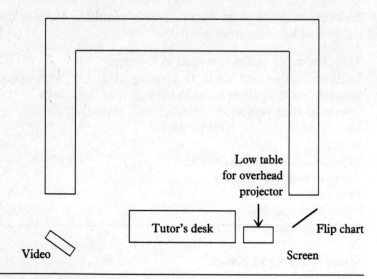

Figure 3A.1   Training classroom layout

(c) Notify persons who must attend seminar of venue, time and programme

A memo is sent to all persons nominated to assist at the exhibition stand, giving details of the training that has been arranged.

MEMORANDUM

To: J. Horsell, P. R. White, F. Peters, N. A. Joly, R. R. Sand, B. Brown, R. T. Brown, S. Sugar, T. Hopkins, F. R. Billy.

From: Peter Trant, Manager Engineering Services.

Date: 15 November

Subject: Training Seminar for International Technology Exhibition, Olympia.

Because of the importance of the International Technology Exhibition to company progress, a training seminar has been arranged for all participating.

Please attend punctually on 17 November at the Keswick Conference room. The day's programme is as follows:

9.00–9.45	Introduction. What an exhibition achieves.
9.45–10.45	Administration
Coffee	
11.00–12.30	Product knowledge
Lunch	
1.30–3.00	Face to face with exhibition visitors
Tea	
3.15–4.15	How to generate good PR
4.15	Commitment

As manager of the engineering services department, you are competent to cover the technical aspects of product knowledge in addition to all other sessions. For political reasons you decide to invite the technical director to conduct the product knowledge session. He accepts the invitation and tells you that he will bring his own handouts and training material with him. Diplomatically, you recommend that his session finishes with a multiple choice test questionnaire, for participants to monitor the extent of their learning.

The programme is sent to the participants, with copies to the managing director, marketing director and technical director.

(d) Design course material

When all the peripheral activities have been dealt with, the course material is designed. The two most important requirements are overhead projector slides and course handout notes.

Overhead slide projectors can be hired or purchased, if not already owned by the company. The slide has approximate dimensions 25 cm × 25 cm. It is an acrylic transparent sheet on
which designs, charts or wording are printed and drawn. There are special pens available for writing on acrylic sheet. Alternatively, Letraset printing can be used. It is usual, but not essential, to have a thin cardboard outer frame to the slide. This makes handling easy. It also enables the name of the slide to be written at the top, on the outer frame, for immediate identification. The projector throws the picture or wording of the slide onto a large screen which all the class can easily see.

For the trainer, the use of the slide allows work notes to be dispensed with. Each item on the slide is a trigger word for the lecturer to deal with a section of his subject.

Overhead slides and course handout notes are prepared for the programme sessions, as follows:

Handout notes		*Figure*
Handout no 1	Prompt sheet	3A.2
2	Course objectives	3A.3
3	What an exhibition has to achieve	3A.4
4	Exhibition administration	3A.6
5	Golden Rules of exhibition stand behaviour	3A.8
6	How to handle technical enquiries	3A.9
7	Greeting exhibition visitors	3A.10
8	Role play grid to monitor Greeting visitors exercise	3A.11
9	Exercise: Rules for achieving the best PR	3A.12
Overhead slides		
Slide no 1	The functions of an exhibition	3A.5
2	The Golden Rules of exhibition stand behaviour	3A.7

(e) Seminar format and procedure

As the participants arrive, invite them to sit anywhere at the U-shaped table. Offer flip chart crayons, which have a thick, bold point, so that each person writes their name on the blank name plate. First names are always used in class.

At the beginning of this course, in turn with other participants, you are invited to stand up and introduce yourself. Say who you are and what you would like to get out of the course: this allows the tutor to get to know his class, and helps everyone to settle into a comfortable working relationship.

The subjects you should cover are:

Name

Position in the company

How long you have been working in the company

Previous experience of exhibitions

What you would like to learn from this course

Anything that causes you apprehension

Figure 3A.2   Prompt sheet – Handout no 1

1   Programme for introductory session

The most important contribution of this session is to remove participant apprehensions, and to settle everyone into a comfortable working relationship. Although all the participants are from the same company, it is unlikely that they have more than a casual relationship.

1.1   Handouts and slides are arranged neatly on the lecturer's desk. The manager who is conducting the training introduces himself.

1.2   Starting at one end of the table, participants are invited to stand up, in turn, and introduce themselves. The prompt sheet handout is there for them to use if they wish. When they have said all that they wish to say, or if they dry up, they just sit down.

1.3   Handout no 2 is selected for distribution. Before giving it out, the lecturer says: 'Seminars and courses have to be about something. We cannot just chat indiscriminately. So I

have written some objectives. It is our intention to meet these
objectives by the end of the seminar.

'When I give them to you, please read the objectives care-
fully. Put a tick against the objective that is most important for
You, and a cross against the objective that is least important.
Never mind what the person next to you does.'

By the end of the course participants must be able to:

- describe the administrative arrangements for attending the
  exhibition
- complete the documentation procedures relating to the
  exhibition
- greet visitors to the stand in a relaxed professional manner
- use questioning techniques to identify visitor needs
- deal effectively with obstreperous visitors
- answer technical questions.

Figure 3A.3   Course objectives – Handout no 2

'When you have done this, I am going to go round the class
and record on the flip chart the objectives that are most
important for you, and those that are least important.' This is
a good pointer to how the class thinks.

1.4   Distribute handout no 2: Course Objectives. Whilst class
is reading and marking their handouts, draw a vertical line
down the centre of a flip chart page. On the left hand side
write in capitals Most Important. On the right hand side write
Least Important. Underline each. Preferably use different
coloured crayons. The more colours that are used the more
stimulating it is to the class.

Make sure that the class has understood the instructions,
and when they are ready, write on the flip chart the numbers
of the objectives selected as most and least important. Do this
for each person. Comment on the similarity or divergence of
opinion within the class.

1.5   Comment on the timetable. Each person has received a
copy in the memorandum sent. If it had not been sent, the
timetable would be distributed as a handout.

Stress that the timetable is flexible. It is designed to incorporate everything participants need to know to represent Satellite Communications at the exhibition. However, if the class is involved in a session and it is fruitful, the session does not have to stop because the timetable says so. What is important is that we achieve our objectives.

1.6 'What are the functions of an exhibition stand? Why do we participate?' Next there is an exercise, to find an answer to those questions. As these words are spoken, overhead slide no 1: The Functions of an Exhibition is displayed on the screen – base sheet and overlay 1 only. Distribute handout no 3: What an Exhibition has to achieve.

In syndicate groups, answer the following questions:

(*a*) What are the main functions of an exhibition?
(*b*) What is the order of importance of exhibition functions, starting with the most important? Give reasons
(*c*) Which function is helped most by training?
(*d*) What are the principal obligations of personnel manning an exhibition stand?

Appoint a speaker in your syndicate to present your findings to the group.

**Figure 3A.4   Exercise: What an Exhibition has to achieve –
Handout no 3**

Divide class into syndicate groups of two, three or four persons. Tell them to arrange their chairs in a huddle so that they can discuss the exercise problem together. The exercise has three parts, as set out in the handout:

(*a*) Decide what activities and aims constitute the main functions of an exhibition
(*b*) Arrange the functions in order of importance
(*c*) Decide which function is helped the most by the seminar training.

Allow about fifteen minutes for the class to reach their conclusions. Meanwhile, draw the base pie-chart outline of exhibition functions, as illustrated on the overhead slide (Figure 3A.5), on a flip chart.

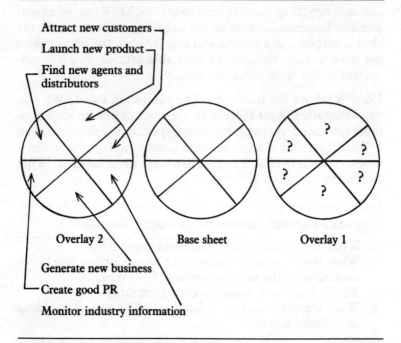

Figure 3A.5 Overhead slide: the functions of an Exhibition

1.7 Ask for the attention of the class. Invite one syndicate to present their findings, and write the function names that they give in each segment of the circle. Ask other syndicates how they differ or whether they agree, and lead a group discussion. In turn, write each syndicate's findings in the circle segments, using different colours.

1.8 When discussions are completed, remove overlay 1 of the overhead slide. Replace with overlay 2. Lead further discussion on the differences or similarities, between class interpretation of major exhibition functions and the ones that you have presented.

Remember that it is valuable, with this and with every session, to design a safety valve, or escape route, in case the designed material is used up too quickly. With experience, a lecturer 'feels' how long material lasts in class. Nevertheless, sometimes groups do not cooperate, or ask or answer questions,

Exhibition administration booklet

Figure 3A.6   Exhibition administration – Handout no 4

and time goes too quickly. For this session, a relevant escape route is as follows:

'One of the important functions of an exhibition is to gather industry information.' Staying in the same syndicates, prepare a checklist advising the class how best to gather industry information. Write the brief, in capitals, on a flip chart. Always make sure that a brief is provided when exercises are set, either by writing it on a flip chart, or by giving out a handout. Supply each syndicate with a page of flip chart paper and a crayon.

Instruct them to write their checklist on the flip chart sheet. When the task is complete, a member from each syndicate comes to the front and presents their list to the class. Blu Tack is particularly useful for fixing up loose flip chart sheets. Hand the participant a pointer when he or she comes to the front. Holding something is valuable in overcoming nervousness. It also serves the function for which it was intended, of pointing.

2   Administration session: 9.45 am to 10.45 am

2.1   Distribute handout no 4: Exhibition administration. Run through arrangements, rota, expenses, parking, cover for absence from work, emergency contact arrangements, overnight accommodation, entertaining, stand documentation, admission cards, stand badges, etc.

Ensure that everyone concerned knows where they are supposed to be, when, and what is expected of them.

3 Product knowledge: 11.00 am to 12.30 pm

3.1 This session is led by the technical director who is responsible for handouts and visual aids.

4 Face to face with exhibition visitors session: 1.30 pm to 3.00 pm

4.1 The session commences with an exercise. Before the class assembles write the following brief on a flip chart page.

Brief: prepare The Golden Rules of Exhibition Stand Behaviour.

It is best to cover the page until it is time to disclose it. Otherwise, some impact is lost. Mix up the syndicate groups so that class members work with different people from their morning syndicates.

Advise class that the session begins with an exercise. Disclose the brief. Allow about ten minutes to complete.

4.2 On a fresh flip chart page write the rules that the syndicates have evolved. Take one rule from one syndicate. Move to

---

The Golden Rules of Exhibition Stand Behaviour

- Prepare for daily use, checklist of display equipment and materials
- Arrange adequate supplies of literature, visiting cards, record pads and pens
- Always be well groomed
- Always be smiling and cheerful when talking to visitors
- Always be courteous
- Record contact name, company, and customer's interests before visitor leaves stand.

Figure 3A.7   Overhead slide: The Golden Rules of Exhibition Stand Behaviour

another and take the next rule. Move to each syndicate in turn until all rules have been transcribed. For the actual writing, a person from the class who writes neatly can be invited to come to the flip chart. This gives the lecturer greater control. It also involves a participant to a greater extent than just listening.

4.3 Display overhead slide (Figure 3A.7) The Golden Rules of Exhibition Stand Behaviour. Distribute handout no 5, giving the rules shown on the corresponding overhead slide.

- Prepare for daily use, checklist of display equipment and materials
- Arrange adequate supplies of literature, visiting cards, record pads and pens
- Always be well groomed
- Always be smiling and cheerful when talking to visitors
- Always be courteous
- Record contact name, company and customer interest before visitor leaves stand.

Figure 3A.8   The Golden Rules of Exhibition Stand Behaviour – Handout no 5

Lead discussion on difference or similarity between class effort and the rules provided.

4.4   Discuss each of the Golden Rules, in turn. Ask a volunteer to define what is meant by 'Be courteous'. Discuss. Obtain consensus from class as to the meaning, and the requirements necessary to obey the rule. Invite other volunteers, or nominate participants, to work through each of the rules in like manner. Allow approximately ten minutes.

4.5   Distribute handout no 6: How to handle technical enquiries. A brief is described in the handout. Distribute a sheet of flip chart paper to each syndicate. Allow ten to fifteen minutes for preparation. Monitor performance so that if all are finished early the session can continue. Meanwhile, set up video camera, recorder and monitor for use in the next session.

Customers making technical enquiries are seeking an informed response. Stand helpers with some technical knowledge can be helpful to a limited extent. In syndicate, decide on procedure, when technical experts are engaged elsewhere.

Record your decisions on a flip chart sheet for discussion in class. Use the space below to prepare master checklist of items helpful to you.

Checklist: How to handle technical enquiries

●

●

●

●

**Figure 3A.9   How to handle technical enquiries –
Handout no 6**

When ready, syndicates present their lists. Leave each list on the wall in front of the class, so that participants can select ideas to record their own master checklist.

4.6   Distribute handout no 7: Exercise: Greeting visitors to an exhibition stand. Describe to class what they are to do. The brief is as set out on the handout. Ask for first volunteer to be recorded on video film. Tell volunteer to leave the classroom whilst a visitor is being briefed. Nominate a person to be a visitor. With the help of the class, create an identity for the visitor. Write the identity and needs of the visitor on a flip chart as they evolve, so that the person role-playing the visitor can make notes if necessary. Recall volunteer.

In turn, members of the class play roles of a meeting between a visitor and a helper on the stand. The meeting is recorded on video tape for playback analysis. Persons playing the role of visitor are provided with an identity.

Remember, the purposes of the exhibition are to generate business and goodwill.

Use the space below to make notes, helpful to your role in greeting a visitor.

Figure 3A.10   Exercise: Greeting visitors to an Exhibition Stand – Handout no 7

4.7   Distribute handout no 8: Grid to monitor greeting visitors to an exhibition stand. Inform class that participating in the role-play exercise by specifically monitoring the performance is as important as the role-play itself. The grid is to be used. Observers evaluate performance by ticking each aspect of behaviour that is perceived.

4.8   Use camera to record the role-play. Cut after three or four minutes so that, allowing for replay and analysis, there is time for others to participate in the exercise.

4.9   When the first role-play has concluded, ask the actors how they thought they performed. Invite class to comment constructively. Rewind film. Replay and stop playback frequently. Invite comments from class on performance. In this way the whole class is involved. Even if there is insufficient time for everyone to practise in front of the camera, all are closely involved with what to do and what to avoid.

5   How to generate good PR: 3.15 pm to 4.15 pm

5.1   Advise the class that the session examines ways of generating good PR for Satellite Communications. Each person has

	Cheerful disposition	Confident	Authoritative	Well informed	Competent	Other
Helper 1						
Helper 2						
Helper 3						
Helper 4						
Helper 5						
Helper 6						
Helper 7						
Helper 8						
Helper 9						
Helper 10						

Your contribution in monitoring the performance of others is constructive and valuable.

Place tick in appropriate column each time person role-playing manifests the particular attribute.

Figure 3A.11　Grid to monitor exercise: Greeting of visitors to an Exhibition Stand – Handout no 8

the task of translating those ways into the specific context of manning the exhibition stand.

Distribute handout no 9: Exercise: Rules for Achieving the best PR. Write the following brief on a flip chart.

Brief – Part 1: Working in pairs, write down all the different ways in which you would like Satellite Communication to be described; for example, innovators, market leaders and so on. Allow ten to fifteen minutes. When the class is ready call out a person to transcribe the findings onto the flip chart.

In class all the different ways in which you would like Satellite Communications to be described are being considered, and written on a flip chart. The descriptions are numbered.

Your task then, working in pairs, is to develop a set of rules to achieve all the numbered items listed.

Copy the numbers of the items onto a piece of paper. After each rule is developed, cross off the numbered items to which it refers. When all the numbers are crossed off the set of rules is complete.

Your rules, and those prepared by the others will be shared and discussed together. From the total effort copy down, in the space below, the rules that are going to help you promote good PR in the future.

Rules to promote good PR for Satellite Communications

1

2

3

4

5

Figure 3A.12   Exercise: Rules for achieving the best PR – Handout no 9

5.2   Record all the descriptions produced by the syndicate pairs. There is likely to be overlap and repetition. When the list is complete, number each item.

Write the remainder of the brief on the flip chart.

Brief – Part 2: Working in the same pairs, develop a set of rules to achieve all the numbered items listed on the flip chart page.

Advise class to copy the numbers onto a piece of paper. Each time a rule is created, the numbered items to which it relates should be crossed off. In this way, methodically, no PR items are going to be left out.

5.3 Transcribe the rules developed by each pair to a fresh flip chart sheet in front of the class.

There will again be overlap and repetition. Lead class discussion on the rules that have been produced. Eliminate unsuitable rules. Class then copies the rules remaining and accepted, onto handout sheet no 9 (Figure 3A.12).

5.4 Go round class. Ask each person in turn to interpret the rules governing good PR in respect of their own participation at the exhibition.

6 Commitment session

6.1 Ask class to refer back to handout no 2: Objectives (Figure 3A.3). Read each objective in turn. Ask class to confirm whether that objective has been achieved in class.

6.2 Ask class 'What apprehensions do you have for the forthcoming exhibition?' Discuss. Ask each class member in turn.

6.3 Ask class 'What plusses are you going to take to the exhibition?' Again, go round class, asking each person in turn. Discuss.

6.4 Summarise achievements of class. Compliment them on their performance. Encourage all to participate successfully at the exhibition.

4 Creating and maintaining good customer relations

Before reading this chapter, try to answer the test questions given below. The answers will emerge in the chapter itself and appear in a summary at the end.

QUESTIONS

How can customer relations be turned into *good* customer relations?

How does the service manager lay his plans to promote good customer relations?

What should a publicity campaign for customer service describe?

How can the sales force help good customer relations?

What objectives for a joint salesman/engineer training session would help to promote good customer relations?

With what current events does the successful service manager concern himself/herself?

Chapter 4 synopsis

- The difference between good and bad
- Managing change
- Something to shout about
- Planned help
- A training programme
- The nuts and bolts of good service management

THE DIFFERENCE BETWEEN GOOD AND BAD

Question How can customer relations be turned into good customer relations?

Good customer relations do not just happen. They are the product of careful planning, close control, and the ability to adapt to changing circumstances and needs. When good customer relations are achieved, supplier and customer benefit, and each derives a commercial advantage. Both are satisfied.

Customer relations start at the beginning of the personal selling cycle when an offer is made to a potential customer. At this stage the service department has not physically entered the scene. Marketing promotion, publicity, and personal selling are in direct contact with the customer. Customer relations have but a distant presence in the client's perception of the following contributions:

- training in equipment operation
- reliable installation
- prompt service response time
- availability of replacement parts
- professionalism of service engineers
- competitive cost of after sales service
- reliability of equipment.

The client awareness of these aspects of service is not always on a conscious level. Priority is often given to equipment purchase, or rental costs, production capability, size, operator requirements, product component supply and storage problems.

If the client makes the decision to use the company equipment, then awareness of the need for installation service, training and after sales service is suddenly highlighted. Planning to bring the promise of immaculate service attention to the awareness of potential customers, right at the outset, is persuasive and sensible. It structures the foundation for achieving good customer relations.

MANAGING CHANGE

Question How does the service manager lay his plans to promote good customer relations?

In many companies the service manager is a second-class citizen. Marketing and services are often disregarded. Little attention is paid to the contribution of the service department, as there is minimal service involvement in marketing planning. It is by no means an ideal situation. Organisations are often slow to include contributions from the service department at the planning stage.

Before considering the stages in creating good customer relations in the market place, there is a preliminary step to be undertaken. The service department manager must become a first-class citizen. This preliminary step can be a trade off within the company. In return for parity of management and planning say, the service department can make an enormous contribution to company progress. If *you* find yourself in the situation described, negotiate *now*. The following list provides negotiating tools of considerable strength:

- Back-up service support for demonstrations and promotions
- Extended warranty periods
- Free maintenance trial periods
- Guaranteed round the clock response time
- Profit contribution as a profit centre
- Equipment usage training
- Regular market research feedback
- Alternative service support options
- Customer needs related advertising copy.

From a position of strength, the service manager now approaches the problem in hand.

Place tick in appropriate box	VB	B	Fair	G	VG
1 What is your experience of after sales service back-up?					
(a) company	☐	☐	☐	☐	☐
(b) other	☐	☐	☐	☐	☐
2 What is your experience of equipment reliability?					
(a) company	☐	☐	☐	☐	☐
(b) other	☐	☐	☐	☐	☐
3 How reliable is replacement parts back-up?					
(a) company	☐	☐	☐	☐	☐
(b) other	☐	☐	☐	☐	☐
4 What disruption is caused by service visits to					
(a) production	☐	☐	☐	☐	☐
(b) personnel activities?	☐	☐	☐	☐	☐
5 What is the response time to service call requests?					
(a) company	☐	☐	☐	☐	☐
(b) other	☐	☐	☐	☐	☐
6 What degree of profession-alism is demonstrated by service personnel?					
(a) company	☐	☐	☐	☐	☐
(b) other	☐	☐	☐	☐	☐

Figure 4.1 Customer service needs audit

Place tick in appropriate box   VB   B   Fair   G   VG

7   What degree of technical competence do service personnel possess?

(a) company ☐ ☐ ☐ ☐ ☐
(b) other ☐ ☐ ☐ ☐ ☐

8   How competitive are servicing costs?

(a) company ☐ ☐ ☐ ☐ ☐
(b) other ☐ ☐ ☐ ☐ ☐

9   What is the diagnostic success rate of service engineers?

(a) company ☐ ☐ ☐ ☐ ☐
(b) other ☐ ☐ ☐ ☐ ☐

10   What degree of dedication do service engineers show for your company progress?

(a) company ☐ ☐ ☐ ☐ ☐
(b) other ☐ ☐ ☐ ☐ ☐

Figure 4.1 (concluded)

Stage 1   Customer service needs audit

First, the manager must identify the needs of his customers. They are not all likely to be the same unless the company products are all sold into one narrow customer segment. Research takes the form of questions, which are asked directly of equipment users. Existing customers are likely to cooperate, because any activity directed towards improving the service they get is evidence that the company cares.

Do not assume that new products introduced by the company necessarily carry the same customer service needs as the existing equipment range. New equipment has inventory problems, engineer training requirements, and an increased call rate during the familiarization period. Depending on the industry, equipment downtime ranges from mere inconvenience to dramatic production difficulties.

The data secured from the audit is the platform for the marketing of the service back–up. Figure 4.1 is an audit questionnaire for customer service needs.

Stage 2 Publicity campaign for customer service

SOMETHING TO SHOUT ABOUT

Question What should a publicity campaign for customer service describe?

A prime marketing objective for the company products relates to satisfaction of the customer's needs. The objective for customer service is no different. The customer has to know that when buying or renting equipment from the company, he or she is also receiving first class back-up service. The precise objectives stem from the feedback gathered in the customer service needs audit.

Marks and Spencer plc invite all their customers to complain at any time. Before any purchase is made, every potential customer knows that the product can be returned without argument or query. The Marks and Spencer customer service needs campaign is excellent. Hand in hand with the company's emphasis on product quality is the integral back-up of a commitment to a valuable customer service.

One arena of competition in the market place is price, which can be a self destructive area. Sometimes there are differential advantages due to economies of scale or technological leadership. But when prices are cut what is left? Quality is eroded. Customer service offers a much wider arena in which to be competitive. Non-price competition is not bounded by the single factor of money. Customer service is a value added component. It is part of a package of benefits that make up the total product. There are many examples of value added packages for ordinary everyday products and services:

- washed and scrubbed potatoes in a bag
- protective plastic covers for the driving seat of the serviced car
- dry cleaning delivered to the home
- wallet and itinerary with the purchase of an airline ticket.

The customer service value added component differentiates the product. The greater the service, the greater the competitive differential. But being different has a cost. The end product is a quality level. Marketing decisions have to be made, as to what level at what cost. The decisions rest on the data of what the customers need, and what the competition is offering. The following factors are relevant:

● Spare parts back-up

Sophisticated inventory control systems are able to ensure an effective parts delivery as and when required. There are subordinate problems of inventory management for the service manager in terms of level of service targets, economic order quantities, re-order levels. From a marketing point of view, supplying parts when they are needed, at the time they are needed, is an important component of a quality package.

● Short response time

For the customer there is optimum production capacity when there is minimum downtime with the plant and equipment. Downtime is a function of four factors:

1 number of service calls
2 time taken by engineer to repair equipment
3 response time necessary for engineer to call following customer's request
4 time required to carry out preventive maintenance work.

The response time is usually measured from the time of the client call to the time of the engineer's arrival at the customer's premises. In normal circumstances only the standard working hours of 8.30 am to 5.00 pm are taken into account. Evening and weekend time do not enter into the calculation unless specifically agreed.

Figure 4.2 shows a response time distribution for a workforce of engineers. In area A the customers receive a relatively

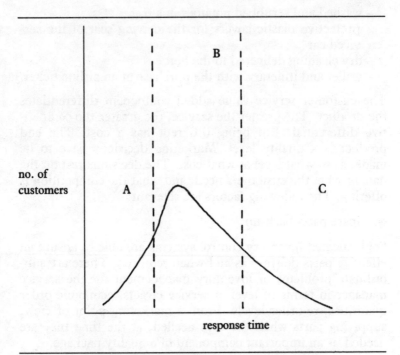

no. of
customers

response time

Figure 4.2   Response time distribution

fast response time. The average response time is for customers
in area B. There is a tail. It is in area C that customers have the
longest response times.

There are a number of ways of improving the situation. The
simplest is also the most expensive, which is to increase the
sales force. This achieves shorter average response times overall but has to be balanced against lower individual productivity,
and higher costs. An alternative way to reduce response time,
subject to industry requirements, is for the engineers to carry
sub-assemblies, which they exchange, instead of effecting
repairs on site. Another alternative is in the planning of
engineer territories to secure an overlap that reduces maximum territory distance to be covered by any engineer. By
manipulating the resources available to him, the service
manager is able to promise a given response time. A short
response time and a response time that is guaranteed twenty-
four hours around the clock, is a very potent tool of the

marketing mix. The psychological advantages to a customer of a guaranteed short response time can greatly exceed the financial cost to the service manager of making the service available.

● Extended warranty

The implication of an extended warranty offered by a manufacturer is the reliability of the equipment. During a warranty period customers are not charged maintenance costs except for consumable items, and in industries where this is possible, it is an effective marketing tool. Many electronic components have a low failure rate that is significantly different to that of electro-mechanical components. Marketing capital is made of the fact that the manufacturer is able to make the commitment of an extended warranty. Where the product itself is subject to mass advertising in the media, the advertising ripple effect on consumers exerts an extended influence.

● Technical advice

Most companies welcome technical expertise that is complementary to their own skills. As specialists, technical experts can involve themselves in the problems of companies. Solving problems sells equipment and lays the groundwork for commercial relationships.

● Operator training

Operator training has a double benefit. It ensures that the customer derives maximum benefit from operating the equipment and eliminates service calls due to equipment abuse. Sound operator training, backed up by easy-to-follow operating and maintenance manuals, transfers minor maintenance problems and troubleshooting to the customer's own service personnel. Trouble-free plant translates into savings and profits for factory managers.

● Equipment demonstration

For sophisticated equipment, demonstrating on customer site can involve complex installation and service resources, and costs are likely to be substantial, but demonstrating a product is one of the best ways of selling. The best way of all is allowing the customer to operate the equipment, not just to see it in action. Saab, the motor car manufacturers, claim that some eighty per cent of their new cars are sold to previous owners. Planning to install equipment on a client's factory floor for a trial period is a sound marketing tactic in appropriate circumstances.

The factors described are important to customer relations, so they should be featured hand in hand with the promotion of the product. Historically, service management has not always had involvement in marketing planning, and service departments have coped, or not coped, with ad hoc calls from their own resources. Management without planning is a costly business where profits can be lost, but the biggest victim of all is customer relations.

Stage 3　Sales force dialogue

PLANNED HELP

Question　How can the sales force help good customer relations?

Ideally, service engineers and salesmen should communicate freely. Each should have a realistic perception of the other's job and of the demands each has to meet. The salesman is proud of his drive and initiative. The engineer takes pride in technical competence and tenacity. Their roles are different, but each contributes to the dynamic progress of the company. There may sometimes be jealousy or discontent. The sales force may consider that engineers are insulated from the pressures that salesmen have to face, and engineers may see the income structure, with commissions and bonus payments as unjust and a cause for some jealousy. The rights and wrongs are rarely thrashed out, but the two forces have to achieve a working harmony.

Good customer relations demand more than 'peace' between salesman and engineer; dialogue is essential, and they must support each other. With the customer as a starting point, marketing publicity has to proclaim that the company cares, even before equipment is purchased, as well as saying it afterwards. The salesman has to continue the message. Good customer service is a value added benefit, and as such has to be sold. Benefits do not sell themselves.

It rests with the service manager to build a reciprocal relationship between engineers and salesmen. The following actions are helpful:

- social gatherings
- competitive sporting events
- including salesmen and engineers on the circulation lists for the others' internal memoranda
- encouraging engineers and salesmen to exchange leads and warnings of impending large production runs
- shared training to highlight the problems of each others' tasks. A half day is ideal but certainly not less than about two hours. The objective of the training being to introduce each to the other's work pattern.

A TRAINING PROGRAMME

Question What objectives for a joint engineer/salesman training session would help to promote good customer relations?

The principal objectives of a joint training course are (a) to identify the obligations and pressures of each profession leading to a closer understanding, and (b) to develop techniques to promote the value added benefits of good customer service along with the product.

The training aspect is of paramount importance. A model timetable and manual are given in the appendix at the end of this chapter (pages 80–92).

Stage 4 Managing the day to day service function

THE NUTS AND BOLTS OF GOOD SERVICE MANAGEMENT

Question With what current events does the successful service manager concern himself/herself?

The targets of the service manager are very different to those of the sales manager. Sales are concerned with events, and every new sale attracts plaudits and praise. Service is concerned with non-events, and the longer the period in which there is no untoward call by customers the more effectively the service department is doing its job. Effective service means that company equipment in use by customers is wrapped in a cocoon of service efficiency and support. Achieving the top level means a lot of hard work, and customer orientation is the starting point.

Customers

Initial customer contact for the service department is likely to be at the equipment demonstration or during a trial installation on the client's premises. A contract is placed, and the equipment is installed and is left in working order. At this point the manager should make contact on behalf of his department. There are important messages to give to the customer and a letter is appropriate for this, preferably preceded by a personal visit. The messages are:

(a) an introduction.

(b) a statement of dedication from the service department for the smooth operation of the company equipment.

(c) a statement of the average and maximum response time for service calls.

(d) an offer to supply equipment operator training to customer engineers or reserve operators.

(e) a statement of performance periods after which routine maintenance is recommended.

(f) the advantages to the customer of buying a maintenance contract.

(g) an open invitation for suggestions of ways that the service back-up can exactly match the customer's specific needs.

The next area of concern for the service manager is holding regular staff meetings.

Meetings

Ideally meetings with all present should be conducted daily. Often this is not feasible because some of the engineers move straight into their territory from home, and even with meetings held once a week, there are still problems due to urgent calls that require immediate attention.

At the staff meeting the following subject items are covered:

Technical problems It is useful to refer to any ordinary malfunction. Problems and solutions are discussed. Preventive actions are adopted where appropriate.

Staffing problems Holiday rotas, absence because of illness and domestic commitments are dealt with.

Company news Company progress, staff changes and promotions, company plans, product development, technological development; all newsworthy items are essential contributors to departmental morale.

Any other business There is an opportunity for an engineer to raise any point that he wishes discussed in open session. It is also expedient for a manager to be available before or after a meeting for an engineer who wishes to discuss a problem privately.

Another important area of management attention is making the engineers want to work.

Motivation

The good manager strives continuously to sustain the ambition, energy and loyalty of his team. Praise is a powerful tool, as are bonuses and perks, and the manager needs to monitor engineer performance. He does this by observation, and by analysis of record sheets. Repeat calls, excessive time on routine maintenance work, forgotten tools and spare parts, are particular indicators that all is not well.

An engineer starting on his patch after induction training is excited with the challenge of meeting equipment problems. Privately, there are apprehensions, such as failure to diagnose machine faults, inadequate parts or tool supply, disruption of customer environment. After some time in the field, experience gives the engineer confidence, and he becomes familiar with the usual equipment malfunction problems and has the experience to diagnose the less frequent bugs. It is to the experienced engineers that the manager must offer the crutch of motivation, hand in hand with confidence boosting to the inexperienced.

The fourth main area of concern for the service manager is how he organises his department.

Departmental logistics

Information storage

For engineer movement there is basic and variable information. Basic information consists of:

(a) customer details
(b) equipment data.

Variable related information is:

(c) date and time of customer call
(d) reported fault
(e) time of engineer despatch
(f) time of engineer arrival
(g) cause of fault
(h) time to repair
(i) any other work performed
(j) parts supplied.

The information is provided by the engineer in a number of ways; electronically, by report form or by telephone. The format is a function of the volume of data and the decision-making uses to which it is to be put. Reporting is an essential discipline for an engineer.

Inventory control

Inventory is investment. Some spare parts are needed rarely, others frequently. The management of inventory translates directly into increased or diminished profitability. Precise records must be kept on part movement volumes. Usage patterns govern the stocking levels, which are also influenced by the supplier quantity discount structure, and the supplier's lead time.

Work allocation control

Records are kept on computer, on a card system, or by another convenient method, of how, where, when and for what purpose work is allocated. A measure of the effectiveness of control is the customer response time. Another measure is cost; travel costs, staffing costs and inventory level costs to support the number of engineers employed.

SUMMARY

Question How can customer relations be turned into good customer relations?

Answer Good customer relations are achieved as a result of careful planning, promotion and control.

Question How does the service manager lay his plans to promote good customer relations?

Answer The service manager's task in promoting good customer relations is made up of four clearly defined stages:

stage 1 customer service needs audit
stage 2 publicity campaign for customer service
stage 3 sales force dialogue
stage 4 managing the day to day service function.

Question What should a publicity campaign for customer service describe?

Answer A publicity campaign for customer relations should describe the added value benefits with which a product is enhanced by an effective service department.

Question How can the sales force help good customer relations?

Answer The contribution of the sales force is selling the added value benefits of customer service along with the product.

Question What objectives for a joint engineer/salesman training session would help to promote good customer relations?

Answer The principal objectives of a joint engineer/salesmen training session should be (a) to identify the obligations and pressures of each profession leading to closer understanding, and (b) develop techniques to promote customer awareness of the value added benefits of good customer service.

Question With what current events does the successful service manager concern himself/herself?

Answer The manager of a successful service department is concerned with (a) customer events, (b) conducting regular departmental meetings, (c) engineer motivation and (d) departmental logistics.

APPENDIX TO CHAPTER 4

Model timetable and manual for joint engineer/salesman training course

Timetable

9.00–9.45	Introduction Exercise: A typical day
9.45–10.45	What makes a person tick Qualities for the job. Work pressures. How to succeed
Coffee	
11.00–11.30	Case studies A, B, C and D Role play exercises in service engineer routine
11.30–12.00	The personal selling cycle Exercise: Understanding the salesman's role
12.00–1.00	Helping customer relations Exercise: The importance of the salesman's help
End	

Tutor's notes and class handouts follow for each of the sessions in the timetable

Introduction

Tutor's notes

1   Advise class that the objective of the joint training session is to integrate the activities of service and sales. Each makes a vital contribution to good customer relations and the profitability of the company. If they work together there is synergy. The whole is greater than the sum of its parts.

1.1   Exercise. Divide class into syndicates of two or three persons. Each syndicate is either made up of salesmen or engineers. Do not mix. Distribute handout no 1. It instructs

Working in syndicate groups, your task is to devise a day's work that you think is typical for an engineer/salesman. Select the occupation that is not your own. Place the diary grid below beneath an acrylic sheet, so that your complete day's schedule can be shown to the class on the overhead projector.

6.30–7.00
7.00–7.30
7.30–8.00
8.00–8.30
8.30–9.00
9.00–9.30
9.30–10.00
10.00–10.30
10.30–11.00
11.00–11.30
11.30–12.00
12.00–12.30
12.30–1.00
1.00–1.30
1.30–2.00
2.00–2.30
2.30–3.00
3.00–3.30
3.30–4.00
4.00–4.30
4.30–5.00
5.00–5.30
5.30–6.00
6.00–6.30
6.30–7.00

Figure 4A.1   A typical day – Handout no 1

the class working in their syndicates to prepare a diary of a typical day for a salesman or an engineer. Salesmen devise the day for an engineer and vice versa. Allow ten minutes. Distribute a sheet of flip chart paper to each syndicate. The timetable is to be written on the sheet for subsequent presentation to the class.

1.2 During exercise write the brief for next exercise on flip chart. Do not let class see brief yet. The wording is:
Brief – Prepare list of all things that can go wrong in the course of the engineer/salesman working day. Select the occupation that is not your own.

1.3 When syndicates are ready, allow them to present, in turn, their diaries to the class. Encourage salesmen and engineers to correct any misapprehensions. Draw conclusions of gaps in knowledge of how colleagues in a company work.

1.4 In same syndicates invite class to undertake exercise of 1.2. Display brief. Allow about ten minutes. When class is ready, invite syndicates in turn to call out their lists. Write on a flip chart. Invite one member of class to do the writing. There will be overlap when the lists of each syndicate are added up. Finally the tutor has two lists, one for sales and one for engineers. Lead class discussion on problems and opportunities.

In syndicate prepare the diary of a typical day that occurs in the working week of an engineer or salesman. (Figure 4A.1) Choose the profession that is *not* your own.

Work together in your syndicates. Do not obtain help from nearby friends. Write your timetable on the acrylic sheet that your tutor provides.

Elect a member of your syndicate to present your findings to the class.

What makes a person tick

2 Advise class that in this session the objective is to find out more about each other.

2.1 Distribute handout no 2: Personal qualities. It tells class to prepare a list of the six personal qualities that are helpful to an engineer or to a salesman. They are to be ranked in order of importance. Allow ten minutes.

2.2   When ready, inscribe lists from each syndicate on flip chart. There are likely to be more than six qualities for each profession. Lead class discussion on comparison. Restrict discussion to 10.15 am at latest.

In syndicates:

(a)   prepare a list of the six personal qualities you consider essential for a salesman/engineer. Choose the profession that is not your own.

(b)   rank the qualities in order of importance.

(c)   decide what is the minimum number of qualities that should be present for a person to be good at his or her job.

Give reasons for all your decisions.

Figure 4A.2   Personal qualities – Handout no 2

2.3   Give class new exercise.
Brief – prepare the Golden Work Rules for the perfect salesman/engineer
   Write brief on flip chart for all to see. Distribute flip chart sheets for syndicates to inscribe their rules. Allow ten to twelve minutes.

2.4   Invite syndicates to present. Careful control is needed so that all syndicates have the opportunity to make their presentations. Salesmen may be more articulate. They must not be allowed to dominate discussions.

Case Studies

Tutor's notes

3   There are four short case studies for service engineers. They are to be role-played by salesmen. Invite volunteers. Control the length of each to a maximum of five minutes.

You are despatched to a customer where an ABC machine was installed two months ago. It has had an excessive number of feeder calls. Another engineer who went there four weeks ago tells you that he is sure they are not using the feeder within specification.

When you arrive you cannot find much wrong with it. Then the customer says 'The two previous mechanics obviously didn't fix it. What makes you think you can do any better?'

How do you respond?

Use the space below to plan for the role you are acting.

To help you, ask yourself these questions:

What do I want to achieve?
What does the customer want?
What else am I likely to be asked?
Do I know what the customer's real problem is?
Am I effective as a service engineer?
How is the problem to be solved in such a way that both parties are satisfied?

Figure 4A.3   Case Study A – Handout no 3

You have just finished a call and are immediately despatched to repair a new installation. It is the first in a newly opened territory. Your supervisor has stressed the importance of this machine. It is being watched. A good reputation will attract more business in the area. The machine is in a market town some distance from the service centre.

The agreed response time is four hours maximum. When you arrive the customer says 'This won't do at all! It's three hours since I called for service. The sales rep assured me that it would never take more than two hours to get a service man here.'

How do you react?

Use the space below to plan for the role you are acting.

To help you, ask yourself these questions:

What do I want to achieve?
What does the customer want?
What else am I likely to be asked?
What are my reactions?
Do I know what the customer's real problem is?
Am I effective as a service engineer?
How is the problem to be resolved in such a way that both parties are satisfied?

Figure 4A.4   Case Study B – Handout no 4

One of your machines, installed three months ago, just won't settle down. You keep getting called back for classic operator related faults. You can never find anything wrong. The operator, a prickly individual, is fully confident of his ability. 'I have been working on this type of machine for eight years. I don't make mistakes.' Your conversations with the operator become less friendly. He eventually complains to the manager that you have been patronising.

A supervisor takes the next call. He finds a badly crimped connector on a paper path switch which causes occasional paper jam symptoms. The next day your supervisor sends for you.

Where did you go wrong?

Use the space below to plan for the role you are acting.

To help you, ask yourself these questions:

What do I want to achieve?
What does the supervisor want?
What else am I likely to be asked?
What are my reactions?
Do I know what the customer's real problem is?
Am I effective as a service engineer?
How could the problem be solved in such a way that everyone is satisfied?

Figure 4A.5   Case Study C – Handout no 5

The customer is manager of a copyshop, one of a large chain. All have the company's latest, biggest machine. The manager has a reputation for placing calls for no good reason. Sometimes he just wants the machine looked over before a period of heavy work.

You are despatched at 4.00 pm on Friday. The traffic is bad and you get there at 5.00 pm. You had hoped you would be nearly home by this time for your small son's birthday party.

You discover no fault with the machine. It transpires that the manager did have some trouble when he placed the call, but realised it was an operating fault that he subsequently rectified. 'I was too busy to cancel the call. However, as you are here, you can give it the once-over, can't you?'

How do you cope with this?

Use the space below to plan for the role you are acting.

To help you, ask yourself these questions:

What do I want to achieve?
What does the customer want?
What else am I likely to be asked?
What are my reactions?
Do I know what the customer's real problem is?
Am I effective as a service engineer?
How is the problem to be solved in a way that is acceptable to both parties?

Figure 4A.6   Case Study D – Handout no 6

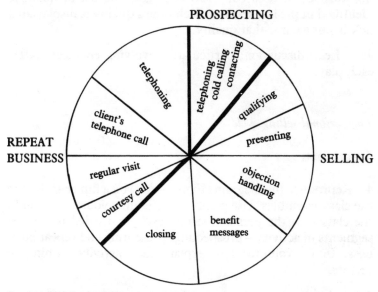

In syndicate decide :

a Which of the personal selling segments – prospecting, selling or repeat business – makes the most important contribution to the personal selling cycle?

b On which single specific *selling* aspect would you concentrate if you wanted to coach a weak salesman to improve his performance quickly?

c In what way would a salesman's performance be improved by a course in telephone selling?

d Next to securing a sales contract, what is the biggest contribution a salesman can make to his company?

**Figure 4A.7   Exercise: The Personal Selling Cycle –
Handout no 7**

3.1   Class monitors each role-play. The method of monitoring must be structured. Class is to take the list of qualities identified in the last session. Each time a quality is displayed, a tick is put against that quality.

3.2   Lead discussion, particularly involving engineers, after each play.

The personal selling cycle

Tutor's notes

4   Reproduce the diagram (Figure 4A.7) on a flip chart before the class assembles. Use plenty of different colours. Explain to the class how the personal selling cycle is divided into three segments of activity – prospecting, presenting and repeat business. Invite volunteers to explain each activity within the sectors.

4.1   Divide the class into syndicates. Distribute handout no 7. Invite class to work through the exercise described. Allow fifteen minutes.

4.2   Discuss findings. Always allow engineers to present their answers first and involve salesmen in following discussion.

Helping customer relations

Tutor's notes

5   For this session syndicates are mixed to contain both engineers and salesmen. In advance draw three circles on a flip chart. One at the top, one in the middle and one at the bottom. The title is Contributory Factors to Good Customer Relations. Next to the top circle write 'For Customer', next to the middle circle, 'For Salesman' and against the bottom circle 'For Engineer'. From the mid point of each circle draw five dotted radius lines dividing each circle into five segments.

5.1   Distribute Handout no 8: Good customer relations. Tell class that in their new syndicates, they are to identify the factors contributing to good customer relations, from the points of view of customer, engineer and salesman. Perhaps the factors are identical in each case? There are not necessarily five. You have arbitrarily drawn five sectors, but the class is free to alter this as they see fit. Allow fifteen minutes.

5.2   Let each syndicate call out their factors, in turn. Write in on circles on the flip chart. Evaluate and discard inappropriate factors, but carry out in a way that makes clear that it is the class discarding the factors and not the tutor. Lead class discussion on findings.

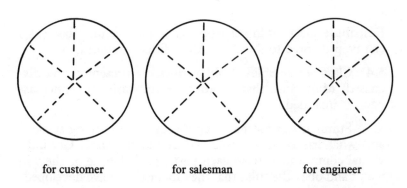

for customer   for salesman   for engineer

The circles above have been arbitrarily divided into five component segments.

In syndicate identify the factors that you consider reflect the view of the customer, salesman and engineer. If you consider that the total number of factors in any circle is more or less than five, alter accordingly.

Figure 4A.8   Contributory factors to good customer relations – Handout no 8

5.3   Divide class back into closed syndicate groups of salesmen and engineers. Distribute handout no 9. Class is to prepare the Golden Rules for Achieving Good Customer Relations. The engineers write the rules from the point of view of engineers. The salesmen do the same from their point of view.

In class you have identified the factors that contribute to good customer relations. How best are they to be employed?

In syndicate prepare the Golden Rules for Achieving Good Customer Relations.

Engineers prepare the rules for engineers. Salesmen prepare the rules for the sales force.

Write on the flip chart sheet provided.

Figure 4A.9   The Golden Rules – Handout no 9

Distribute sheets of flip chart paper so that the inscribed rules can be presented to the class. Allow fifteen minutes.

5.4   Class reassembles. Golden rules are presented and discussed. Make sure that appropriate emphasis on service aspects is included.

5.5   Summarise what has been discussed in training session, and what has been achieved. Go round the class. Get individual commitment from each participant that he or she will adopt and obey the rules that they themselves have developed.

5 When the customer has a grievance

Before reading this chapter, try to answer the test questions given below. The answers will emerge in the chapter itself and appear in a summary at the end.

QUESTIONS

What is the simplest action for an aggrieved customer?

What kind of institutional help is available in the UK for the customer with a grievance?

What pressures exist on a company, outside of law, to change its pattern of commercial or industrial behaviour?

What is the mechanism of arbitration open to a customer and a company in dispute?

In England, is there a difference in law as it applies to services as compared to goods?

Chapter 5 synopsis
- The first step
- A range of options
- Consumer pressures at work
- Finding a solution
- Consumers and the law

THE FIRST STEP

Question **What is the simplest action for an aggrieved customer?**

From time to time every manufacturer and supplier of goods and services encounters a customer with a grievance. The grievance may be real, or imagined, but attention to the problem is necessary. Customers seek redress in a variety of ways.

Refund. The significance varies for the supplier depending on the nature and price of the goods and whether the supplier is the actual manufacturer, distributor or retailer.

Repair. Repairs reflect cost to the supplier. The terms under which the goods or services were supplied are pertinent. So also are possible loss of future business and damage to a PR image.

Replacement. The supplier evaluates the problem of dealing with returned goods against benefits accruing from satisfying the customer's demands.

Staff disciplinary action. Opportunities for personality conflict between customer and staff occur most frequently when services are supplied. It is likely that the customer is tied to the supplier and is a potential source of future business. Another factor for consideration is that genuinely abrasive staff are able to upset more than one customer.

Apology. Commercial considerations are outweighed by personal ones. If an apology is received the customer is usually content to let matters drop.

Three other categories of customer bring grievances to suppliers – political activists, cranks and 'professional' complainers.

Political activists. Such people are articulate, able and energetic. Any action that they take is likely to be well planned with effective back up. Example: harassment of a company where objection is taken to the employment of specialist South African personnel.

Cranks. The demands of cranks fall outside the normal range of customer needs. Usually there are strong views that conflict with management's perception of how it should run its own business.

'Professional' complainers. This small, vigorous group exists in many industries. Their objective is to secure supplies of placatory goods or services at little or no cost. An example is the customer who returns a small portion of uneaten pizza to a pizza manufacturer, complaining that, when cooked, it had a funny taste.

The ground rules for suppliers and manufacturers dealing with customer complaints are simple and straightforward. They can be condensed into a single rule: *The Customer is of Paramount Importance*. Whether the demands are unreasonable, or punitive in terms of cost, the customer in his or her customer segment, represents potential future business. Such business must be wooed.

A RANGE OF OPTIONS

Question **What kind of institutional help is available in the UK for the customer with a grievance?**

There are very many organisations equipped to help the customer with a problem. They include government departments, government-sponsored agencies, local authorities and voluntary bodies. Some are concerned with making and improving policies that help the consumer. Others are concerned with the implementation of existing policies. Some give advice, some help the consumer obtain redress for specific grievances.

Many government departments, such as the Ministry of

Agriculture, Fisheries and Food, and the Department of Health and Social Security, are involved in consumer protection. However, the main official body in this field is the Office of Fair Trading. Set up as a result of the Fair Trading Act 1973 and headed by the Director General of Fair Trading, the OFT is ultimately responsible to the Secretary of State for Trade and Industry. Its objective is to protect both consumers and industry against unfair trading practices. It keeps a lookout for traders who persistently commit offences or break their obligations to their customers, for example, builders who fail to carry out promised repairs, or car dealers who sell defective vehicles. It produces a range of leaflets explaining consumers' rights in simple language, often reinforced by cartoon-style drawings.

Another activity is checking on the fitness of traders who provide credit facilities, and the Office of Fair Trading issues licences to approved concerns. Guidance for the traders, including safeguards for the consumer, is published under the Consumer Credit Act.

The Director General of Fair Trading, through his departmental organisation, collects information about trading practices. If they are thought to be unfair he may recommend changes in the law, or other remedies. Policy is usually formed at central government level. It results from the influence and recommendations of various pressure groups – some of them government-sponsored such as the National Consumer Council, some independent like the Consumers' Association.

Implementation of policy occurs at local level. The agencies concerned are local authority trading standards and consumer protection departments. Their officers have powers to warn and to prosecute. Local agencies that advise the consumer, but do not help in obtaining specific redress, include Citizens' Advice Bureaux, Consumer Advice Centres, local consumer groups and law centres. Most libraries also contribute by supplying the leaflets issued by the Office of Fair Trading.

CONSUMER PRESSURES AT WORK

Question What pressures exist on a company, outside of law, to change its pattern of commercial or industrial behaviour?

One of the most significant contributions arising from the Fair Trading Act 1973 is the encouragement of trade associations to police their own activities. The mechanism for this is the Code of Practice. While the Office of Fair Trading is able to make recommendations, the Code is designed and implemented by the representative members of the trade association.

Over twenty Codes of Practice have been negotiated with the Office of Fair Trading. The industries include electrical appliances, motor cars, travel agents, shoes, laundries, furniture and mail order trading. Membership of a trade association imparts credibility to a member, in commercial terms. The emblem or badge is displayed prominently on letter heading and on the company's premises. Observance of the code is normally left to the individual member, but some trade associations check to ensure that members do follow the Code. Sanctions against members who break the Code range from expulsion to a fine to social displeasure. To ensure that the public at large know of the Codes of Practice many pamphlets and posters are available free of charge from the Office of Fair Trading. The following example relates to Car Repairs and Servicing.

Codes of practice have been produced by the Motor Agents' Association, the Society of Motor Manufacturers and Traders Limited, the Vehicle Builders' and Repairers' Association Limited, and the Scottish Motor Trade Association Limited, which give the following protection:

Cost

You should be given a firm quotation for the job if possible, or at least an estimate in writing. In either case it must be clear whether VAT is included and the rate of charge. Should dismantling be necessary for the purposes of an estimate or quotation (for instance, lifting out an engine) this must be pointed out to you and the charge for this service made clear. Once any job is under way and it appears to the garage that the price quoted is likely to be exceeded by any significant amount (for example, if they come across further difficulties) the garage should ask your permission to continue.

Guarantee

Repairs must be guaranteed for a specified time or a number of miles against failure due to poor workmanship. In addition Vehicle Builders' and Repairers' Association members under their code must guarantee their repair work for not less than six months or 6,000 miles' use from the date of repair. The repair guarantee will normally be extended if your vehicle is off the road due to faults or because further work has to be done as a result of previous defective work. Furthermore, the repairer should permit any unexpired period of guarantee on repairs to be transferred to a new owner of the car.

Care of the car

The garage must take adequate care of your car and other possessions, and should tell you about any additional defects found, even if they have nothing to do with the work in hand.

Invoices

Any invoice should give you full details of work carried out, and parts used, the amount and rate of VAT, the date of repairs and the milometer reading at the time.

If you feel you have not been treated fairly and that the garage has not honoured the code, you should complain to the particular motor trade association of which the garage is a member. An arbitration service is provided under the codes, under which a member of the Institute of Arbitrators will be appointed to study the papers and make a judgment of your complaint.

FINDING A SOLUTION

Question   **What is the mechanism of arbitration open to a customer and a company in dispute?**

Arbitration in its simplest form is where an independent impartial third party provides a solution to a dispute, both parties to the dispute having agreed to abide by the decision of that third party. The dispute can arise from the sale of goods, or from the supply of a service. It can be a claim for payment of debt, or for damages arising from negligence. There is no bar whatsoever to the nature of a dispute that seeks to go to arbitration.

In the county courts, defended money claims that do not exceed £500 are automatically referred to arbitration. No solicitors' costs are involved as both parties are able to present their own case for hearing.

How to Sue and Defend Actions Without a Solicitor, published by HMSO states:

> The purpose of arbitration is to enable people to have small disputes resolved in an informal atmosphere, avoiding so far as possible the strict rules of procedure usually associated with court proceedings. This does not mean that rules are not observed because the object of all court procedure is to protect the interests of each party to an action and to ensure that the case is tried fairly. Nevertheless the formalities are kept to a minimum and you should have no difficulty in handling your own case.

Claims over £500 up to £5000 in the county courts can still go to arbitration, if both parties so desire, but solicitors' fees are allowed.

In industries where a Code of Practice has been established there is invariably provision for the appointment of an arbitrator in the event of a dispute. In a building dispute, for example, claims can be referred for arbitration to the President of the Institute of Chartered Surveyors or his elected nominee.

For parties to a dispute, not willing, or able to have recourse to the county courts, or the resources of an industry watchdog, there is a third avenue. It is to seek a solution to the problem through the Institute of Arbitrators. The Institute, formed in 1915, was granted a Royal Charter in 1979. It is a multi-disciplinary body with its members drawn from the law, shipping, building, engineering, banking, insurance, accountancy, commodity markets, etc.

A scale of costs is published by the Institute. Currently, the fee for a Request for arbitration is £75. The Arbitration Rules, 1981 edition state: 'By way of guidance, the rates for arbitrators'

fees on 1 March 1981 fall, in most cases, within the following range:
Time for meetings or hearings (including travelling time and time wasted by late postponement or cancellation) – £250 to £750 per day or part of a day. Other time spent on the arbitration – £30 to £100 per hour'.

Parties to a dispute submit documentary evidence supporting their respective claims and counter-claims. With or without a hearing, as agreed between parties, the arbitrator makes his award in writing, setting out reasons for the conclusions that are reached.

CONSUMERS AND THE LAW

Question In England, is there a difference in law as it applies to services as compared to goods?

In England, in respect of services there is judicial disagreement in terms of interpretation. The law has not yet been developed as precisely as the law for the sale of goods.

There are four important statutes likely to be met by the service manager when in dispute.

1   Sale of Goods Act, 1973 as amended by the Supply of Goods (Implied Terms) Act 1983

Services are not covered under this act. However, there is an obligation that a service, whatever it is – looking after cars in a car park or repairing lifts – must be carried out in a proper and workmanlike manner. If it is not done properly, and loss or damage is suffered, it may be possible to claim compensation. But there is no legislation for services equivalent to that of the Sale of Goods Act.

2   Unfair Contract Terms Act 1977

One definition of an exclusion clause is the small print devised to allow companies to provide a substantially different kind of service from that reasonably to be expected of them. Until the late 1970s such exclusion clauses were valid. Provided, that is, that they were brought to the attention of consumers when the contract was struck. Needless to say, the implications of the exclusion clauses were not always explicitly explained.

The Unfair Contract Terms Act 1977 changed the situation. A trader is no longer allowed to restrict or limit liability, or contract out of liability, for death or personal injury which results from negligence or breach of duty.

For claims which do not involve death or personal injury, exclusion clauses are only valid if they are fair and reasonable in the circumstances. Guidelines are laid down in the Act, and are known as the reasonableness test.

1   The bargaining strength of the parties to the contract.
2   Whether any inducement was given to the customer.
3   Whether the customer had an opportunity to enter into a similar contract with other persons without the disputed clause.
4   Whether the customer knew, or ought reasonably to have known of the existence of the exclusion clause.
5   Whether the term excludes or restricts liability if some condition is not complied with, whether it was reasonable at the time of the contract to expect that compliance would be practicable.

Additionally, businesses cannot exclude liability for their own breaches of contract. For example, in a hiring contract such as a video rental, the company who supplies the product cannot use an exclusion clause to remove its responsibility for seeing that the goods are fit for their purpose.

The Act does not apply to insurance, to the sale of houses, to copyright, to trade marks or to company shares. There is, however, a wide range of services, including government departments, local authorities and nationalised industries to which it does apply.

3   Trade Descriptions Act 1968

Under the Act it is a criminal offence for a trader to make materially inaccurate statements about the goods he is selling, or the services he is offering. The offence is punishable by a fine or imprisonment.

There are two categories of statement that can be made about products or services. The first is a 'representation'; the second a 'puff'. A representation is a statement of alleged fact:

'100 per cent nylon', 'unbreakable' or 'two-hour dry cleaning service'. The statement can be proved to be true or false.

A 'puff' is a statement of opinion. The seller or supplier of a service makes exaggerated statements in praise of what is being offered. Examples are, 'the best in Britain', 'saves you pounds' or 'the softest on the skin'.

In theory, the Act should mean that consumers can rely upon the descriptions that are given for the services that they buy. If the tour operator's brochure of the hotel in France says that it is on the beach, then consumers expect that it is so. If it is not so, there can be prosecution under the Act. Unfortunately, the border line between 'representations' and 'puffs' is not always clear.

Although beauty is a personal sense, the concept is universal, so it could be presumed that a statement that a car was 'beautiful' would be a representation. In a Trade Descriptions Act case, it was held to mean that the car was roadworthy. The seller was not portraying a vehicle for a vintage car museum and, the court said, it both meant and was taken to mean that the car was roadworthy. The car was defective, so the seller had applied a false trade description to the goods, and the buyer was entitled to compensation.

In practice the rules for goods and services are different. A service business is liable only if a wrong description can be proved to have been made knowingly or recklessly. In addition certain kinds of suppliers of services are not liable for responsibility under the Act. Estate agents are exempted because houses are not legally either goods or services.

If the buyer of a defective product relies on a commercial puff, he cannot lawfully complain if he suffers loss. If he is fooled by the statement, he can return the goods and demand back the money paid, plus damages for any loss that he has suffered as a result of the misrepresentation. Alternatively, under the Misrepresentation Act 1967, as amended by the Unfair Contract Terms Act 1977, he may retain the goods and claim damages.

4   Unsolicited Goods and Services Act 1971

Under the Act it is a criminal offence for the sender of unsolicited goods or services to make any demand for payment from the recipient. Before the Act was introduced it was growing practice for goods and services to be supplied unasked, with an invoice following demanding payment. Unsolicited supplies of carbon paper to the offices of large organisations is a common example. And inserting telex directory entries is another example of unsolicited services.

The consumers' position has been further protected by the Unsolicited Goods and Services (Invoices, etc.) Regulations, 1975. The notification of price must be clearly shown as free of an obligation to payment. Additionally, there are penalties if the sender threatens to bring legal action, or places, or threatens to place the consumer's name on a black list of defaulters, or invokes any other collection procedure.

If unsolicited goods are received, and you do not agree to keep them, the sender can take them back during the six months that follow. If you have not agreed either to keep or to send back the goods, they become your property after six months. They are then free for you to use or dispose of as you wish. The six month period can be shortened by writing to the sender giving your name and address and stating that the goods were unsolicited. If the sender fails to collect them within 30 days they become your property, but the sender must be allowed reasonable access to collect them.

SUMMARY

Question What is the simplest action for an aggrieved customer?

Answer As a first step, an aggrieved customer enters into a formal dialogue with the supplier of the goods or services that have not given satisfaction.

Question What kind of institutional help is available in the UK for the customer with a grievance?

Answer There is a wide range of organisations concerned with consumer protection. They include government departments, government-sponsored agencies, local authorities and

voluntary bodies. Between them they look after consumers'
and traders' interests in a number of ways: (1) by publishing
information on people's rights; (2) by monitoring trading
practice within an industry; (3) by making recommendations
for changes in legislation.

Question What pressures exist on a company, outside of
law, to change its pattern of industrial or commercial
behaviour?

Answer Voluntary Codes of Practice have been set up within
a number of industries to safeguard and promote the interests
of consumers.

Question What is the mechanism of arbitration open to a
customer and a company in dispute?

Answer For small disputes involving claims under £500 an
arbitration settlement is possible through the county courts.
For disputes where larger sums are involved, parties have the
opportunity to settle their disagreement by the process of independent arbitration through Trade Association appointees,
or through the medium of the Institute of Arbitrators.

Question In England, is there a difference in law as it
applies to services as compared to goods?

Answer Yes. The law as applied to services is not yet as
precisely codified.

Part II
Dealing with the Customer

6 Good and bad communication

Before reading this chapter, try to answer the test questions given below. The answers will emerge in the chapter itself and appear in a summary at the end.

QUESTIONS

What is meant by communication?

Why should service personnel be trained to listen?

What technique can service personnel borrow from personal selling to improve communication with customers?

What are the barriers that company communications must overcome?

Chapter 6 synopsis

- The meaning of communication
- How listening helps
- Using questions skilfully
- Surmounting communication barriers

THE MEANING OF COMMUNICATION

Question   What is meant by communication?

Communication is a process of passing messages. Message signals go from sender to receiver. At the same time, feedback or entirely different messages may be sent from the receiver to the sender. Third parties sometimes intrude and sometimes 'noise' or external forces distort messages. Messages are not only words. Many signals are given before even the first words are uttered, or signals may take the form of a nervous cough, a threatening gesture, a smile, or fidgeting. For true communication all the available signals must be recognised.

Example   The employment interview

An applicant goes into the office of a prospective employer to be interviewed. Normally, in that situation, the interviewer sets out a chair for the applicant to sit on. The chair is placed in a position that is convenient for the interviewer and the interviewee. There is no value in the chair being a long way from the interviewer's desk because the applicant might not hear properly or it may be difficult for documents to be read. Similarly, if the chair is too close to the desk both parties feel crowded.

There are two options for the interviewee:

First, the applicant is shown into the interviewer's office. When invited he or she sits carefully and precisely on the chair and waits for the interview to begin. This is reasonable behaviour and is quite acceptable. It does not show the applicant to be weak and subservient; if anything, it suggests that the applicant is courteous and respectful.

Secondly, the interviewee enters the room. When invited to sit down, he or she picks up the chair and moves it into a new position, a few centimetres away. The applicant then looks around the room, sits comfortably and waits.

Up to that point there is very little change in the physical situation. With this applicant however, very much has been said without a word being uttered. By his or her action the applicant has given body signal messages that are very clear. The message is 'Thank you for the interview situation. I welcome this meeting between us. I am going to listen to see if there can be a useful outcome. I have arranged myself comfortably. You may now go ahead'.

Communication messages do not have to be long and complicated: a single gesture tells as much as a long prepared speech. For the service engineer the non-verbal signals most likely to be encountered are those reflecting stress or apprehension. Such signals are threatening posture, rapid hand movements, accelerated speech, frequent changes of posture, and pacing up and down. Some signals, such as repeated looking at a watch, transparently indicate the apprehension of the person involved.

It is valuable for an engineer to appreciate all the signals that are given. When there are indicators of particular stress the engineer is able to reinforce the care, attention and concern for customer interests. No special training is needed for this. It is sufficient for the engineer to be on the lookout for non-verbal 'tell-tale' signals. An occasional competition, say, once every six or twelve months, provides the team with motivation to watch out for the signals.

Competition How many non-verbal signals do our customers use? On Monday, Tuesday and Wednesday next week, watch out for their signals. Record them. Make a list giving the meaning of each signal. A prize will be awarded at the Friday meeting for the engineer submitting the longest list.

The competition is equally applicable to any industry where service is provided face to face. Non-verbal signals are given out even on the telephone – but they are more difficult to perceive. The signals take the form of a giggle or a sigh, fast talking or sudden silence or rapid breathing. With practice they are recognised instantly.

HOW LISTENING HELPS

Question Why should service personnel be trained to listen?

The most important part of communication in the working day is listening, and the least important is reading. The sequence of activities is reading, writing, speaking and listening. With much to hear it is very easy for a service engineer to restrict what he does hear to the subjects immediately related to his work.

Effective listening requires practice. Relevant words and sounds are highlighted, and irrelevant conversation and noise shut out. There are many examples in everyday life, like the mother of the small child who hears her baby's cries above the highest level of noise. The housewife identifies the drip of a kitchen tap against radio and conversation. The engineer himself instantly detects the slightest change in the hum of his equipment engine – a change that others cannot recognise even when they try to hear it.

If the constraints to listening are removed the service engineer hears much that is of interest to his company. Management and operatives alike are usually ready to talk about impending change and about exciting events scheduled to occur in the near future. This feedback is relevant to the engineer's company for two reasons: (1) extra pressures may be put upon the service department resources, and (2) the information is a useful lead to the sales department for the supply of additional equipment to the customer or to companies associated with them in a new venture.

It is possible to devise exercises to improve listening. As an example, a tape recording is prepared with a story of commercial or industrial interest. Some irrelevant facts and activities are included in the passage that is read. The participants are told of the principal subject area that they are about to hear, so that everyone is conditioned to concentrate on the given subject. After hearing the tape, recall is tested by questions on what has been heard. The extent of the recall of the irrelevant material is evaluated.

An alternative exercise is for the passage described above to be printed. The class then work in pairs. One reads the passage to the other. Again the extent of the recall is tested, and the results evaluated.

It can be argued that learning effectiveness in respect of listening comes from the discussion of the subject and the degree of reinforcement that follows. Perhaps the simplest training approach is a discussion followed by the development of a checklist. Engineers in the classroom are divided into syndicates, with the following Brief:

'In syndicate, develop a checklist of actions to improve listening capability when working with customers.'

The important action to be achieved is that participants lift the fences and filters that they impose on their own hearing.

The following checklist items can be added to any that engineers produce for themselves:

Improvement of listening checklist

Place tick in appropriate box   YES   NO

● Am I relaxed when the customer is talking
to me?   ☐   ☐

● Am I confident that I can deal with any
technical problem likely to be met?   ☐   ☐

● Do I know how the customer's business
is doing?   ☐   ☐

● Do I know of any impending changes in
the customer's production or personnel?   ☐   ☐

● Am I responsive to conversational gambits
on customer premises?   ☐   ☐

● Am I interested in the customer's needs
and problems?   ☐   ☐

If the answer to each question is Yes, OK. If No, do something about it!

USING QUESTIONS SKILFULLY

Question **What technique can service personnel borrow from personal selling to improve communication with customers?**

Listening is an important activity, but it is passive. When customers are speaking they can be helped along. The customer can be prodded with questions. Salesmen use questions to qualify prospective customer needs. There are five types of questions. That is all that is needed.

Questions to assist communication flow

1 Neutral Closed

Invites a Yes or No answer. It may give information but it does not encourage further conversation. The most important use is as a pointer in conversational direction.

Example: Are you going to diversify next year?

2 Neutral Open

The questions usually commence with 'What?', 'Why?' or 'How?' The questions invite the person being asked to talk about the subject in terms of his own priorities. No constraints are imposed at all.

Example: What is the value of training in communication?

3 Neutral Leading

Neutral leading questions often commence with 'When?', 'Where?' and 'Who?' These questions narrow the answer down more precisely than with a neutral open question but still leave freedom of response, within the set limits.

Example: When do customers call at the factory?

4 Loaded Minus

This question very much leads the answer that is given. Loaded minus questions often start with 'You don't ...?', 'You wouldn't ... ?' The question is useful to a salesman wishing to reinforce his selling position.

The contrived situation is helped by the person asking the questions shaking his or her head.

Example: You wouldn't buy from manufacturers supplying shoddy parts, would you?

5 Loaded Plus   Loaded plus questions pay outrageous compliments to guide the answer along a favourable path.

Example: With your years of experience, would you agree to our photographing you for our magazine, as 'Mr Skilled Operator'?

In a training situation, the questions are disclosed to the class one at a time. After an example of the way that the question is used is given, participants are asked to take a piece of paper, and, individually, write down two examples of the question used in their own work. The tutor then goes round the class to hear each question. The process is repeated for all questions.

Questioning, and improved skills in listening are tools for service personnel to use. It is not intended that they take over and diminish the service function. The objective is to make two-way communication with the customer as effective as possible. When it is, the customer achieves the fullest operating efficiency, and the company is helped through feedback to plan for continuing service back-up.

SURMOUNTING COMMUNICATION BARRIERS

Question What are the barriers that company communications must overcome?

The most enduring communications from the customer service manager to the customer are likely to be operating and maintenance instructions. Most commonly they are written in a manual, but some instructions are printed and attached to the equipment, and others are painted on a flat surface on the equipment.

Figure 6.1 illustrates the communication process. Between the starting point of the concept and the communication message received by the customer there are barriers.

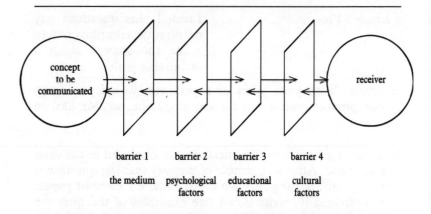

barrier 1	barrier 2	barrier 3	barrier 4
the medium	psychological factors	educational factors	cultural factors

Figure 6.1   Barriers within the communication process

The Concept. The service manager knows what has to be done to install or assemble, operate and maintain the equipment. This knowledge has to be communicated to the customer. It is not straightforward. Who is the customer? Is the customer a man or woman, old or young? Is the equipment designed for children? For example, with a microcomputer, a child may be able to operate the computer but not be able to unpack and assemble it. Does the customer speak English well? Is he or she well educated?

Barrier 1. The medium. Is the message to be printed? Are illustrations desirable to reinforce or to substitute for the written message? In what format should the message be? Is a booklet most suitable? If so, what size? How many colours should be used? If the message is to be an integral part of the equipment, where is the most convenient position?

Barrier 2. Psychological factors. The manager conveying the message may have a different life style and background to that of the operative, or the individual using the equipment. Some customers for example, may not realise that all electric current should be turned off before the inside of the equipment is touched. For some customers this elementary precaution must be spelled out. Another example is assembly. First the base is set down. This logical step may not be apparent to everyone.

Barrier 3. Educational factors. Language that is too complex may not be understood. The manager understands it because he is writing it, but he should entertain the possibility that the customer does not understand. Syntax must be simple and words must be short. Wherever possible operating instructions should be visual as well as written.

Barrier 4. Cultural factors. There are many ethnic groups living in the United Kingdom. Some work in factories where, as users of equipment, there are possible language difficulties, and, especially when there are hazards to safety, the instructions must be visual in sign language to overcome difficulties of interpretation.

Receiver. The sender's message, surviving distortion from the medium, filtering and screening from the barriers, arrives for interpretation by the receiver.

With good communication, there is no difference between the message at the start of the communication process, and the message at the end. To achieve this, there are certain checks the service manager must apply:

1   The language must be pitched at a level low enough for all to understand. Sentences must be simple. Words must be short.
2   Some words have different meanings for different groups of people; for example, high, large and frequent. Values must be defined precisely.
3   Abbreviations and initials which are standard jargon within an industry must be clearly defined. Outsiders are not always familiar with such terms.
4   The message must be tested for comprehension on many different types of customer.
5   Wherever possible, instructions must have illustrations to reinforce the written word.
6   'Danger' and 'Warnings' with their messages must stand out in a striking way.
7   Layout should follow certain guidelines:

- Use typographical 'colour' such as bold and display type, italics, subheadings to make the page more attractive.
- Establish a rough balance of black and white space on the double page.
- Balance the pages by having the top margin less deep than the bottom and outer margins wider than inner margins.

If the service message is communicated in the form of a manual care must be taken to protect the manual. A stiff cover is useful. A plastic envelope to contain it is highly recommended. With usage the manual often becomes dirty and bent. Words get stained and obliterated. When this happens communication is distorted.

SUMMARY

Question **What is meant by communication?**

Answer In simple terms communication is the process of passing and receiving messages.

Question **Why should service personnel be trained to listen?**

Answer With training, pertinent customer information is perceived and remembered.

Question **What technique can service personnel borrow from personal selling to improve communication with customers?**

Answer Communication with customers is helped by the use of skilful questioning techniques.

Question What are the barriers that company communications must overcome?

Answer There are psychological, educational and cultural barriers that impede communication between the company and the customer. In addition there may be distortion from the medium through which the message is communicated.

7 Using the telephone

Before reading this chapter, try to answer the test questions given below. The answers will emerge in the chapter itself and appear in a summary at the end.

QUESTIONS

What factors contribute to a good telephone manner?

What separate stages are involved in answering a telephone call to a service department?

What is the best format for do-it-yourself evaluation of performance in answering the phone?

What are the advantages of having rules governing the making of telephone calls?

When vital technical information has to be transmitted by telephone, what training exercise improves performance?

What type of training exercise helps generate good PR from the everyday telephone conversation?

Chapter 7 synopsis

● Professionalism on the telephone
● How to answer the phone
● Improving personal performance
● The benefits of a standardised response
● Passing technical information efficiently
● How to generate good PR

PROFESSIONALISM ON THE TELEPHONE

Question **What factors contribute to a good telephone manner?**

The telephone is regarded by most people in business as a piece of furniture. It is there. Using the telephone is as easy as walking or sitting.

In fact, analysis of the process of speaking on the phone and the different actions of making and receiving calls, identifies specific skills. These skills can be improved by training, just as it is also possible to improve the way we walk, and the way we sit. There are four factors that contribute to a good telephone manner:

1 *Good Communication.* Good communication on the telephone is achieved when messages sent by one party, are received by the other party in the same format as sent, without any distortion. Good communication requires that:

● both parties have the same frame of reference
● both parties agree to use common units and scales
● both parties check frequently to confirm that meanings are clear and as intended
● language is simple rather than complicated. Sentences are short rather than long.

2 *Speaking clearly.* Everyone without organic or psychological impediment can speak clearly, if they want to. Many do not. Sloppy habits have developed, which by repetition reinforce themselves as bad habits. Persons speaking badly rarely know that this is the case. Improvement is achieved by

training. The following checklist of do's and don'ts sets out what is to be done, and what is to be avoided:

Speaking clearly do's

Do hold phone mouthpiece in correct position
Do breathe normally
Do use short sentences
Do speak slowly
Do pause occasionally.

Speaking clearly don'ts

Don't mumble
Don't eat, drink or smoke whilst talking
Don't shout
Don't use jargon
Don't interrupt yourself or others.

3 *Empathy*. Empathy is seeing the situation from the other's point of view. Understanding how the person being spoken to is reacting to what is being said. A traditional example of empathy is for a spectator at an athletics gathering to lift his leg as the highjumper tries to clear the bar.

4 *Courtesy*. Irrespective of the nature of the phone call, courtesy should be an integral part. Courtesy is a social tradition. Lack of courtesy reflects the background of a person and in some cases it is an emphatic indicator of the emotional feelings of the speaker.

HOW TO ANSWER THE TELEPHONE

Question What separate stages are involved in answering a telephone call to a service department?

When the telephone rings, most people pick up the receiver and say 'Hello'. This is friendly, but is not informative.
There are different types of telephone call that need answering:

Type 1 A call from an outside line.
Rule: Respond by giving the subscriber's number.

Type 2 A call from an outside line when the subscriber is a company and no other company uses that line.
Rule: State the company name.

Some large companies employing switchboard operators have a standard greeting:

'01 732 9876 The Browning Tool Company. Good morning.'

Type 3 An internal call on a telephone line dedicated to enquiries from the public.

The switchboard filters the outside calls, so the employee answering knows that it is a person making enquiries.

Rule: Give the department name and invite the enquiry to be stated.
'Sales office. How can I help you?'
'Service department. Peter Delft speaking. What can I do for you?'

Whether to give the name of the person answering depends on the nature of the department and the business. If the caller is a member of the public seeking casual information, a name is unnecessary. If the caller is a customer or potential customer a name is useful. It is a point of reference for the caller subsequently intending to do business.

When a name is given, the surname should be stated, with or without a first name. That is optional. 'Jones speaking' or 'Gavin Jones speaking' are both acceptable. 'Mr Jones speaking' is to be avoided. 'Mr' is a courtesy title that others use. It should not be used by a person to describe himself, unless he is deliberately trying to place distance between himself and the person with whom he is speaking. Custom with regard to Miss, Ms and Mrs is more flexible and it is really up to the woman concerned.

In a service department where a number of people are employed, a standardised procedure for answering incoming calls is productive. The call is divided into stages. For each stage there is a Golden Rule. It incorporates or re-states the rules given above.

Golden rules for answering the incoming call

1 Smile as you pick up the receiver

Smiling is consciously relaxing. A friendly, courteous manner communicates itself to the other end of the phone. Smiling is easy in the morning. By the end of a tiring day it becomes more difficult. If smiling is turned into a habit it is easy to do, and gives benefit to every conversation.

2   Identify the department (and yourself, if appropriate) to the caller

3   Obtain caller's name

The name should be written on a pad, or on a form specifically printed for the purpose. Depending on the circumstances the caller's phone number, company or residence, are taken too. The details must be obtained irrespective of whether the caller launches immediately into the enquiry, begins to outline a complaint, or even commences a tirade of abuse. In the latter case courteously interposing a firm request for the details may contribute marginally to a 'cooling off' process.

4   Establish the caller's needs

If the call is one requiring service attention it is necessary to obtain certain technical details, and other relevant information, as follows:

- Date and time of call
- Name of person logging call
- Equipment
- Equipment specification/model details
- Nature of service request
- Replacement part request
- Name of engineer allocated
- Time of engineer despatch
- Time call completion logged
- Special comments

The information is logged on a specially prepared form, or on a VDU for which an appropriate programme has been written.

Figure 7.1 is a printout copy of a service call feedback programme used by Kodak Ltd to record details of an engineer's report after a service call. The information given by the engineer is translated into planned letter and number codes. From these data records are kept for analysis, and for

---

			SERVICE CALL FEEDBACK			DISPLAY 50
DEPT	064B	EQUIPMENT	SERVICES MANAGE	SERVICE NO	VISIT NO 01	TASK NO 01
COPY	PROD	EQPT/SERV	TRAIN & EDU/SER	TR12345		
	UNIT ID	ACC			EC COVTYP	LAST CALL
01	1462092	P	POSITIONER FOR EKTAPRINT COPIER		M 50	18.05.84
02	1462092	S	SORTER FOR EKTAPRINT COPIER		M 50	01.12.82
03	1462092	X	EKTAPRINT COPIER-DUPLICATOR		M 50	06.08.84

SP. COMMENTS

LINE	UNITID	ACC	JC	LAB	REG	LAB	O/T	LAB	HOL	PURP	SUBSYS	COMP	REM	PC	CALL
01	.....	.....	02	01	2	.....	.....	.....	.....	145	1245	1222	3	02	0?

SPECIAL EXPENSE 1	PRICE	CC	SPECIAL EXPENSE 2	PRICE	CC
....	....	....	....	....	

ESR COMMENTS	....	DEPT CD LAB
	....	00064B .....

PART NO.	QTY	ORDER	CC
437001..................	001	001	.....
....	....	....	.....
....	....	....	.....
....	....	....	.....
....	....	....	.....
....	....	....	.....

NEXT FUNCTION   KEY

			SERVICE CALL FEEDBACK			DISPLAY 50
DEPT	064B	EQUIPMENT	SERVICES MANAGE	SERVICE NO	VISIT NO 01	TASK NO 01
COPY	PROD	EQPT/SERV	TRAIN & EDU/SER	TR12345		
	UNIT ID	ACC			EC COVTYP	LAST CALL
01	1462092	P	POSITIONER FOR EKTAPRINT COPIER		M 50	18.05.84
02	1462092	S	SORTER FOR EKTAPRINT COPIER		M 50	01.12.82
03	1462092	X	EKTAPRINT COPIER-DUPLICATOR		M 50	06.08.84

SP. COMMENTS

LINE	UNITID	ACC	JC	LAB	REG	LAB	O/T	LAB	HOL	PURP	SUBSYS	COMP	REM	PC	CALL
01	1462092	P	02	01	2	00	0	00	0	145	1245	1222	3	02	0?

SPECIAL EXPENSE 1	PRICE	CC	SPECIAL EXPENSE 2	PRICE	CC

ESR COMMENTS		DEPT CD LAB
	....	00064B

PART NO.	QTY	ORDER		CC
437001	001	001	RELAY H40S04C04E02V06	

PRESS 'ENTER' KEY IF THE TRANSACTION IS CORRECT
NEXT FUNCTION   KEY

Figure 7.1   Kodak Ltd. Service call printout

charging to the customer when appropriate. When the engineer telephones, the Service Call Feedback programme is called up on the Despatcher's visual display unit, and entries made in accordance with the information given.

5   Satisfy caller's needs

Give required information
The procedure is straightforward. Information is given and that is an end to the call.

Arrange to obtain and supply information
Most customers expect that the person answering a call has all information immediately available. Customer problems are important to a customer, and usually they are urgent.

If the information is known, the call is straightforward. If not, there are two options. The first is transferring the call to a colleague who can help. The second is to promise to obtain the information, and call back. In the case of calling back, procedure must be very strict. Promises that are not kept create bad business. It is best to present the customer with options giving the customer the choice of action: 'I am sorry, Sir, I need to check the specification of the replacement part that is used in your model. Will you hold on, or shall I call you back?'

Organise appropriate course of action to satisfy the customer's requirements.

Most likely it is necessary to leave the caller whilst help is being organised. Tell the caller what is being done. If it is necessary to put the receiver down whilst the nearest engineer is being contacted, describe the actions that are taking place. Estimate and state the time that is going to elapse before the receiver is picked up again. Lack of customer cooperation arises when the customer does not know what is happening. An example of this is: 'We will certainly arrange for an engineer to call. My own direct link to the engineer pool is engaged, but I can make the arrangements on another line. Please hold on, Sir. I need to put the telephone down whilst I call from the next desk. You will hear nothing for about thirty seconds or perhaps one minute. Is that alright?'

6   Close the call

If information has been given, a courteous goodbye is all that is necessary.

'. . . and the parts numbers are X 7624 and XD 8786. Is that all?'
'Yes. Thank you.'
'Thank you. Goodbye.'

If action has been taken to deal with the customer's needs, it is important to leave the customer with the speaker's name. Even if the person dealing with the phone call passes over responsibility for subsequent action to another, the customer ideally should have a contact point. The company may be large and anonymous. There is much security for a customer in having a name. The customer must know that there is commitment to his or her problem:

'. . . and an engineer will be with you as soon as possible. Thank you Mr Kendrick. My name is Robert Jones, in case you should need to come back to us. Good day.'

7   When action has been promised and delay is occurring, telephone caller to advise the situation

Good customer relations disintegrate rapidly when promised action fails to materialise. Normally, after a call for service there is no intervening telephone call between the reference call and the arrival of the engineer. When it is apparent that a promised schedule is not going to be maintained, one phone call represents the difference between customer tolerance with sustained good relations, and anger and aggression.

'Hello Mr Gail. This is Apex Appliances Ltd. I am calling on behalf of our engineer who is en route for your factory. We have had a telephone call to say that he has been held up in traffic. It is likely to be at least sixty minutes before he can reach your premises. I'm sorry for this delay, but it is due to circumstances entirely beyond our control. We know how important it is for the equipment to be put back into production.'

IMPROVING PERSONAL PERFORMANCE

Question　What is the best format for do-it-yourself evaluation of performance in answering the phone?

Day to day activities are rarely appraised by the persons involved. Their performance is an integral part of routine and habit. It rests with management to initiate an inward look at periodic intervals. A cycle of three months makes sure that performance standards are not allowed to deteriorate. The following checklist helps service personnel to monitor their own performance:

The incoming call checklist

Place tick in appropriate box　　　　　　　　　　YES　　NO

Yesterday:

● Did I smile when picking up the receiver? □ □

● Did I start the conversation by giving the name of the department, and my name? □ □

● Did I establish the caller's requirements correctly? □ □

● Did I give all the required information correctly? □ □

● When applicable, did I arrange to get necessary information and then call back to give it to the caller? □ □

● Did I warn callers first, when I had to put the phone down for a moment in the middle of a call? □ □

● Did I deal with caller's objections and complaints in an effective way? □ □

● Did I close the call properly? □ □

● Did I leave my name with every caller requiring action? □ □

● Did I call back to advise of delay every time
that promised schedules could not be kept? ☐ ☐

If the answer to each question is Yes, the incoming calls are
being answered effectively. If No, do something about it.

THE BENEFITS OF A STANDARDISED RESPONSE

Question **What are the advantages of having rules governing the making of telephone calls?**

Efficient business calls are those that achieve their objectives,
smoothly and easily. Not every call is efficient. Much can go
wrong. The following list gives examples from inefficient calls:

- a wrong telephone number
- no pencil and paper available to record a message
- the conversation made through a mouthful of food
- reason for calling forgotten
- objective of the call not achieved because the conversation
  is sidetracked
- caller gets angry
- caller does not have information to hand that he or she is
  reasonably expected to know.

Golden rules for telephoning out

1 Plan the call first

The telephone number is required. A pen and a pad or piece of
paper should be available. The format and content of the call
are briefly considered, for instance, how to locate the person to
be called, information to be given, information sought, alternative arrangements to be made if required information is not
available. If the call is at all complicated a list should be made
of the subject items to be dealt with.

2 Smile when you pick up the receiver

The habit of smiling contributes to relaxation and courtesy.

3 Introduce yourself and your company

When making a routine call on company business always state the company name. It is helpful to mention your own name too, but this is only essential when there is likely to be further contact.

4 State business

Pleasantries, and social chit-chat are unnecessary. They are appropriate when there is an established relationship between the parties and social bonds have developed.

5 Close call efficiently and courteously

There is a difference between calls made to customers and to others. All are courteous and businesslike. However, calls made to customers must always leave that customer with an image of caring and helpfulness. This does not necessarily apply elsewhere.

PASSING TECHNICAL INFORMATION EFFICIENTLY

Question When vital technical information has to be transmitted by telephone, what training exercise improves performance?

When vital messages are to be passed by telephone, there is no margin for error. In a few years' time the facsimile transmission equipment now available is likely to be commonplace. Meantime, efforts are needed to improve and maintain standards through the traditional communication channels.

As with all training the foremost objective is for participants to develop effective activity patterns and techniques for themselves.

Training objective Improve performance in passing important technical information on the phone.

Training exercise In the classroom, participants are divided into pairs. They are seated back to back and identified as A and B. In front of B there is a desk or table on which to draw or write.

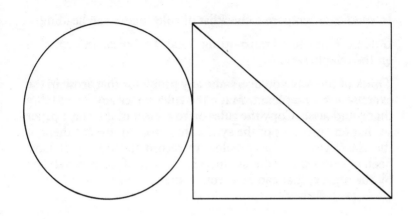

Figure 7.2   Communication exercise drawing no 1

B is equipped with A4 size paper, ruler, pencil and rubber. A is provided with the two drawings illustrated in Figures 7.2 and 7.3.

A's first task is to describe drawing (Figure 7.2) to B. B has to reproduce the drawing. He is not allowed to see it. The only information that is available is the description given by A and the answers to any questions that B asks. Figure 7.2 is a simple drawing to encourage the participants

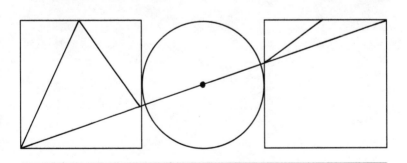

Figure 7.3   Communication exercise drawing no 2

In syndicate, prepare a checklist of rules under the heading:

Golden Rules for Transmitting Vital Technical Information on the telephone.

Think of the way you overcame any problems that arose in the exercise just completed. Make the rules cover any eventuality that could arise. Copy the rules on to a sheet of flip chart paper so that one member of the syndicate is able to present them to the class. Use the space below to record the rules that have been developed by your syndicate, and any of those developed by the others, that can help you in the future.

Figure 7.4   Golden Rules for transmitting vital technical
information – Handout

to relate the designs to everyday objects such as coins and a matchbox.

When the drawing is complete, A and B compare it with the original. Problems and solutions in respect of the exercise are discussed in class together.

The exercise is then repeated using Figure 7.3. In plenary session the tutor asks the B participants and the As what difficulties they had, and what techniques they used to overcome them. The class is then divided into small syndicate groups, ensuring that there is a mixture of participants A and B in each syndicate. The handout (Figure 7.4) is issued, setting the brief for the next part of the exercise. A time of twenty minutes is allowed.

There is likely to be a degree of overlap in the rules produced by each syndicate. Make sure that the following rules are added if they have not been developed in class:

Golden Rules for Transmitting Vital Technical Information on the telephone

- Establish a common starting point

- Establish terms of reference understood and agreed by each side, including units of measure, clockwise or anti-clockwise directions, compass point directions, grid matrix

- Establish a structured programme of working that is acceptable to both sides

- Relate shapes and designs to everyday objects, wherever possible, such as coins, beer cans, matchboxes

- Obtain and give regular frequent feedback.

HOW TO GENERATE GOOD PR

Question What type of training exercise helps generate good PR from the everyday telephone conversation?

Training format

Objective Participants develop techniques to promote good PR whenever they are speaking on the telephone to customers, suppliers and members of the public.

In syndicate, prepare a set of techniques to achieve the PR promotion examples recorded on the flip chart. Write against each technique the number or numbers of the PR example to which it refers. Your list of techniques is complete when all of the PR promotion examples are accounted for. Use the space below to record all the techniques developed by the class that are going to help YOU generate good PR for the company, under the heading:

Techniques to Promote Good PR on the telephone

Figure 7.5   Techniques to promote good PR on the telephone – Handout

Tutor's notes   As the first stage, invite the class, working in pairs, to think of all the ways in which they would like to hear their company described. Give one or two examples: the company is reliable; the company is innovative. Each pair prepares a list on a sheet of paper. Allow the class ten to fifteen minutes. When the lists are complete invite each pair to call out their examples. With the help of a member of the class to do the writing, inscribe the examples from each working pair on a flip chart sheet or sheets. Discuss them, as they are given. Make sure that each is feasible and is not simply a re-statement of a previous example in different words. Number the examples.

As stage two, divide the class into syndicate groups of three or four persons. Distribute handout (Figure 7.5) and describe the instructions that are set out in the handout to the class.

The task is to develop a range of techniques to achieve all the examples of good PR identified.

Illustration   A PR image of the company being reliable. Technique: When being reliable discreetly remind the person being spoken to of the fact . . . 'Hello. Mr Borne? I am calling you back at 3.00 pm as promised. I do not have the information that you want yet, because the managing director is not returning until 3.45 pm. However, I have not waited. We consider it a duty to our customers to do whatever we say we are going to do. I will call you again at 4.00 pm when I should have the information. Is that all right?'

Illustration   A PR image of the company being innovative. Technique: Whenever there is the opportunity, take advantage of the chance to tell customers of the company plans for new products and services: '. . . and the coach arrives at Bristol at 3.00 pm. By the way, Sir, have you ever thought of joining a safari trek? The company is organising a trek across Africa starting on 2 April. It is part of the programme of expansion. Would you like details?'

Record the different techniques on an acrylic overhead projector sheet. When ready, each syndicate presents their work to the class.

SUMMARY

Question **What factors contribute to a good telephone manner?**

Answer There are four factors that create a good telephone manner: 1 good communication, 2 speaking clearly, 3 empathy and 4 courtesy.

Question **What separate stages are involved in answering a telephone call to a service department?**

Answer Answering the telephone involves four separate stages: 1 stating the identity of the person answering, 2 identifying and recording the caller's needs, 3 satisfying those needs and 4 closing the call.

Question **What is the best format for do-it-yourself evaluation of performance in answering the phone?**

Answer To appraise professionalism a simple checklist is quick and effective.

Question **What are the advantages of having rules governing the making of telephone calls?**

Answer A set of rules standardises behaviour so that conformity with those rules ensures that efficient calls are made.

Question **When vital technical information has to be transmitted by telephone, what training exercise improves performance?**

Answer Improving performance in transmitting vital technical information on the telephone is achieved in group training, by an exercise leading to the development of a checklist.

Question What type of training exercise helps generate good PR from the everyday telephone conversation?

Answer The training in development of good PR in everyday telephone conversations has two main elements. First, participants in a classroom situation identify practical examples of good PR. Secondly, the participants develop techniques to introduce such examples on a day to day basis.

8 Face to face

Before reading this chapter, try to answer the test questions given below. The answers will emerge in the chapter itself and appear in a summary at the end.

QUESTIONS

What is the role of the service engineer?

What greeting does an engineer give on arrival at the customer's premises?

How should the engineer dress for visits to a customer's premises?

What are the rules governing behaviour on the customer's premises?

What should the engineer do when equipment abuse is diagnosed?

What common pitfalls must engineers strive to avoid?

What unmentionable things should be mentioned to the service engineer?

What is the procedure for leaving a customer's premises after a service visit?

What personal records are of practical use to the engineer?

Chapter 8 synopsis
- The service function
- The way to begin
- How to dress
- How to behave on site
- One way to help customers
- How to be a better engineer
- Personal hygiene
- How to go away
- An aid to good performance

THE SERVICE FUNCTION

Question **What is the role of the service engineer?**

The service engineer's call has a specific objective: to give technical service. The call is not a social call. Friendly relations between the engineer and the customer may develop over a period of time. The friendship, if it occurs, is despite the relationship, not because of it.

The engineer's visit to customer premises means machine or equipment downtime. The longer the engineer is present, the greater the period when the equipment is not carrying out its intended function. When the equipment breaks down, or malfunctions, there is of necessity a delay before an engineer arrives.

The delay before service attention is provided varies with different industries. In some cases the engineer calls within four hours, and in others, twenty-four or forty-eight hours, or even longer is the minimum period. Pressures develop upon the customer waiting for the engineer to call. If the engineer is later in arriving than expected, customers are often quick to get angry. The customer is not concerned that the traffic is bad or that snow is thick upon the ground. The customer's world is a world where the equipment that he or she needs is not working properly.

A warm friendly welcome is encountered less frequently than irritation and concern. The working environment of the service engineer is potentially hostile. Because of this, the engineer must structure his visit to deal with all customer-related problems in the most effective way.

A machine breakdown does not happen in isolation. In the life cycle of the equipment there are likely to be a number of calls. There are routine maintenance calls. There are repair calls. There are calls to replace parts worn out by wear and tear. Sometimes an engineer is called in anticipation of equipment malfunction, when the customer is preparing for an important production run.

The engineer has to be technically competent and proficient. He must diagnose problems and find solutions. In addition, the engineer needs expertise in industrial relations. He must understand the psychology of stress. He has to be diplomatic and he must be caring. He has to put himself in the position of the customer to understand the difficulties that arise when the equipment is not functioning properly. There is a further dimension. As a representative of his company, the engineer must be polite and appropriately dressed.

THE WAY TO BEGIN

Question What greeting does an engineer give on arrival at the customer's premises?

When an engineer is called to a customer's premises he goes to meet a customer with a problem. The problem takes precedence over everything else. The prime task for the engineer is to find a solution. That is the customer's urgent need. Social chat about the weather, or the local football team is out of place. 'Mr Brown? I am Peter Jenkins, a service engineer for Rediffusion Television. What is the problem?'

The name of the company is given. It is important to give the engineer's name too. In this way if the customer wishes to refer to the call later, it is easy to identify the company representative involved. When the engineer gives his name, it is a matter of personal choice whether the Christian name is given, as with Peter Jenkins, or simply Jenkins. Both are acceptable. The engineer should not call himself Mr Jenkins. As pointed out in the previous chapter, Mr is a courtesy title. It is used by others but should not be used by a person for himself.

HOW TO DRESS

Question How should the engineer dress for visits to a customer's premises?

Customers waiting for service engineers to call often depersonalise the engineer. They wait for an engineer to call, not Peter Jenkins or Jeff Hale. The personality of the engineer is subordinate to his role. The reliable professional engineer can take pride, rather than suffer distress, at being known as the company engineer, instead of by name. Because of the demands of his profession, the manner, the conversation, and the dress of the engineer should reinforce the role that he has to play.

Conventions of dress exist within different businesses and industrial activities. They range from the sober suited to completely relaxed leisure wear clothing. They differ from customer to customer. In the course of his working day the engineer meets both extremes. In order to blend into any environment the engineer's dress should not be obtrusive. While he is working, the engineer intrudes into the customer's workspace, whether factory floor, office or household lounge. Clothing that is loud, or unconventional in other ways, stands out as unusual. It makes sure that the engineer is remembered. But that is not the basis for success as an engineer. An engineer must be remembered as being good at his job.

In reality, how an engineer dresses bears no relationship whatsoever to his skills in providing service, but obtrusive clothes can offend or irritate a customer who is already concerned with equipment that is not working properly, and who does not happen to like unconventional clothing. It is extremely unlikely that the customer will ever comment to the engineer about his style of dress. However, in the occasional situation where there is a continued machine failure immediately after an engineer's call, a 'differently' dressed engineer compounds the problem.

With some equipment, the nature of the work governs the nature of the clothing that is worn. If there is likelihood of grease and staining, protective clothing must be worn. One option for the engineer is to carry an overall that he puts on before attending to the equipment.

HOW TO BEHAVE ON SITE

Question **What are the rules governing behaviour on the customer's premises?**

Customers develop distinct patterns of work behaviour. Whether the customer is in an accountant's office, a zoo, or is a housewife in her new flat, the furniture, the possessions and activities are arranged to an individual pattern of requirements. The engineer has to enter customer space and work within it. The engineer must therefore cause the least possible disruption. If there is to be disturbance and temporary change, the engineer needs to obtain prior permission from the customer.

There is a distinct dividing line. Any activities that fall directly within the professional scope of the engineer, in carrying out his duties, do not need clearance. Removing the back of the equipment to gain access to the working components is a necessary part of the engineer's job. So is dismantling working parts. So is running the machine to diagnose faults. But making use of a nearby table or chair to lay out tools or components needs permission from the client. Moving from room to room to obtain a supply of water, or to dispose of waste and broken materials, needs permission as well.

Checklist of do's and don'ts

Do   Ask permission to make use of or move client's
        furniture
        Ask permission to use client's equipment
        Protect property from damage
        Give warning if undue noise or disturbance is to be
        caused
        Clear away all mess created.
Don't   Wander about client's property without first asking
        Eat or smoke on the client's premises
        Drink tea or coffee without client's express invitation
        Disrupt the work of nearby personnel by chatting
        Use the telephone without prior permission
        Leave equipment and premises in disarray whilst
        leaving the building to obtain parts or tools
        Leave hazardous equipment unattended.

ONE WAY TO HELP CUSTOMERS

Question **What should the engineer do when equipment
abuse is diagnosed?**

One common cause of machine breakdown is incorrect operation. Most manufacturers predict that their equipment is
going to be exposed to inexperienced operators. Within limits
they attempt to protect their equipment against breakdown.
Specific instructions and directions are usually clearly marked.
Despite such warnings, equipment is frequently mistreated.
The actions are not usually malicious. The users do not read
the instructions correctly. Alternatively, they misinterpret
them. Some people are frightened of all technical equipment
and are incapable of understanding the simplest technical,
electrical or mechanical operation.

There is another distinct category of machine abuse. That
comes from the application of excessive force. The reason for
the rough usage is the anger and frustration of the operator.
When a machine fails to operate in the manner for which it is
programmed, or designed, the user is frustrated. He or she

directs the anger and irritation at the machine itself. Levers are pushed, and handles turned with force that is greatly outside prescribed limits. The operator does not usually succeed in making the equipment work, after it has failed, but some of the tension is partly dissipated in the attack on the equipment.

The experienced engineer rapidly diagnoses machine abuse as a cause of malfunction. Making good the equipment, and leaving it in sound working order is a matter of routine. Taking steps to prevent the occurrence is of equal importance, although this may be difficult. The engineer must identify who is responsible for equipment operation. Is there one person in charge, or are there many with access to the equipment when the need arises?

It is the engineer's task to demonstrate the equipment in working order. He must describe what the equipment can do, and what operations are to be avoided. The next step is for the customer to operate the equipment under the guidance of the engineer. When the engineer is satisfied that correct machine operation has been learned by all personnel likely to make use of it, his task is complete.

HOW TO BE A BETTER ENGINEER

Question What common pitfalls must engineers strive to avoid?

Example: Customer A operates a security alarm system. The system malfunctions and he telephones for an engineer to rectify the fault. The manufacturer's control despatcher logs the call, in accordance with company procedure. Before allocating the engineer's visit she becomes involved in two emergency calls.

There is then a road accident immediately outside the office. A pedestrian rushes in to call for an ambulance. Despite strict procedures to prevent such an occurrence, instructions to an engineer to call on customer A are overlooked.

Customer A telephones later. He is very angry. No one has arrived to deal with his equipment.

In this situation, an engineer is finally given appropriate instructions. The despatcher tells him of the events leading to the delay. The engineer knows that he is going to meet a very angry client.

Although the engineer has the training and experience to deal with angry customers, he naturally prefers his customers to be friendly and welcoming. Psychologically, he is at a disadvantage. It is not his fault that the equipment has broken down. Subconsciously the engineer may argue: 'It is not my fault that there has been a delay. It is Margaret, the despatcher who is at fault. If I tell the customer that it is Margaret's fault, he will be cross with Margaret and not with me. Perhaps he will be friendly and pleased with me, because I have told him who is really at fault'.

Much adult behaviour is governed by subconscious motives, even though at a conscious level the validity of those motives is denied. In parallel to the path of the unconscious motives, the engineer can strike an easy degree of friendship with the customer by reacting with him against a malicious third party. The third party takes on various forms:

1 The equipment
If the equipment is at fault, the customer joins the engineer in allocating blame:

'This modern equipment is not what it was like in the old days.'
'This is the Mark III. What can you expect? It is Mark IV that has all the refinements.'
'Look at this component. They make such shoddy parts, these days.'

The engineer has specific technical skills. Most likely, the customer does not have those skills. By giving his opinion of the equipment, the engineer demonstrates his wisdom and authority. The more he berates the equipment, the more he magnifies his power – in his own eyes. From this position of power, as he sees it, the engineer does not leave room to feel threatened by an angry customer.

2 The company
The engineer invites the customer to join him in an 'us' against 'them'.

'Typical. The left hand never knows what the right is doing.'
'What can you expect? Messages are always going astray.'
'Don't be surprised. The messages are always late.'
'It is the despatchers. Those girls never listen.'

By running down the company and his colleagues, the engineer demonstrates the distance between the other wrongdoers and his impeccable self. In the context of all the service calls that are made by his company, the record of mishaps may well be insignificant. The engineer highlights the disasters with which he is familiar.

3 The salesman

Sometimes salespeople say anything to get a sale. It is a fiction that all salespeople lie and exaggerate all the time. With a reputable company supplying branded equipment, heavily supported by media advertising, the scope for the salesman to make wild claims is severely restricted. The salesman who persists in distorting the truth to secure a contract does not stay long with the company. Nevertheless, customers do not always remember word for word what they have been told. Frequently they hear, or believe that they hear, what they want the salesman to say.

'The equipment does not need servicing for the first two years.'
'Labour charges and costs of parts are covered for a year under guarantee.'
'The equipment produces 40 copies per minute.'
'It runs for 200 hours on one battery.'

'What the salesman said' is quoted to the engineer by the customer. Almost always it is at variance to some degree with reality. If the engineer diminishes the credibility of the salesman, it provides a scapegoat. With a ready scapegoat, the customer does not need to turn on the engineer.

4 The customer

Attack is the best method of defence. If the engineer places the customer in the wrong, the customer cannot scold the engineer for equipment failure or lack of communication. An attack on a customer's ineptitude in operating technical equipment quickly reinforces an engineer's position of authority.

'Did you really carry on using the machine when the red light showed?'
'Did you move that lever, even though it clearly said "Do not touch"?'
'Why did you overload the drying tray?'

These examples show that allocating blame to the equipment, to the company, to colleagues, to the salesman who sold the equipment and to the actual customer, gives a form of protection to the engineer's self image. It is very short-term protection. The customer's confidence is rapidly eroded. Customer dissatisfaction spreads rapidly to colleagues, family and friends. It translates quickly into corrective action. The reputation of the company and its products is damaged.

The engineer must not pass blame – even where it is justified. The day by day task of the engineer – hand in hand with carrying out technical work to a high standard of competence – is to reinforce the company image. Carrying out repairs is not enough. The engineer has to see that customers avoid placing unnecessary strain and pressures on the equipment. The engineer must always be loyal and supportive to his company and their products.

Sometimes the company or their products are actually at fault. The engineer must be sympathetic. He must have empathy with the problems of the customer. Caring about the customer's disrupted production run, even working late if asked to set it right, is a contribution the good engineer makes to his job. Passing blame is much easier than accepting it. Shouldering the responsibility for mistakes of colleagues is one of the hurdles to be overcome by the good service engineer.

For help in avoiding the pitfalls, the following checklist should be regularly used:

Checklist for use after week's visits

Place tick in appropriate box   YES   NO

- Did I refrain from blaming the equipment?   ☐   ☐
- Did I refrain from blaming the salesman?   ☐   ☐
- Did I refrain from blaming the company?   ☐   ☐

- Did I refrain from blaming my colleagues? ☐ ☐
- Did I check that the customer and his staff knew how to operate the equipment effectively? ☐ ☐
- Does the customer know exactly what the equipment can and cannot do? ☐ ☐
- Did I leave the customer's premises tidy? ☐ ☐

If the answer to each question is Yes, OK. If No, do something about it!

PERSONAL HYGIENE

Question **What unmentionable things should be mentioned to the service engineer?**

Washing, bathing, cleaning teeth, changing underwear, are personal habits shared by all. The cabinet minister, the service engineer, the deep sea diver and the post office clerk all wash and change clothes. Habits vary, but no one intentionally offends through bad body odours.

The working conditions of the service engineer are not always ideal. Space is cramped, and mealtimes are irregular and such conditions can lead to perspiration smells and to bad breath. No one tells a person that he has bad breath. No one says openly 'you stink of sweat'. The person is just avoided.

Engineers should be aware of the offence that can be given from working diligently and hard. Awareness of the problem brings its own solution.

HOW TO GO AWAY

Question **What is the procedure for leaving a customer's premises after a service visit?**

The engineer's prime duty is to keep the customer's equipment in good working order. Other tasks go hand in hand with high technical competence. There must be no untidy mess left on the customer's premises, furniture and equipment. All waste materials must be removed and all dirtied surfaces wiped clean. Even if the equipment is dirty from the client's own neglect, it is helpful if the engineer cleans this too, before leaving. It is unlikely that the task is written into the engineer's responsibilities. Cleaning up for the client, without comment, is one of the benefits an engineer offers his client, even though technically it is not his task. Being helpful and being caring are necessary companions to the routine work of supplying service engineering.

When the work space is clean and tidy, the engineer then needs confirmation from the customer that the work has been carried out. Most companies provide documentation with a space for the approval signature of the customer. It is not sufficient just to tell the customer that the equipment is now working satisfactorily. The customer is asked to operate the equipment. If incorrect operating procedures have been the cause of machine failure the engineer monitors customer performance, to make sure that it is correct.

Checklist for leaving client's premises

Place tick in appropriate box   YES   NO

● Have I cleared away all waste materials?   ☐   ☐

● Have I reinstated customer's furniture and
possessions to their original state?   ☐   ☐

● Have I wiped all surfaces clean?   ☐   ☐

● Have I checked that operating procedures
are understood and practised?   ☐   ☐

● Have I secured customer's signature of
approval for work carried out?   ☐   ☐

If the answer is Yes, OK. If No, do something about it.

AN AID TO GOOD PERFORMANCE

Question   What personal records are of practical use to the engineer?

With experience, the engineer learns that particular machine malfunction patterns are tied to specific customer segments. When a customer calls for service, he or she usually describes what has happened to the equipment. The customer does not always diagnose the cause of the problem. Often it is not known. Being able to anticipate the cause of equipment breakdown in advance is helpful as the engineer is then able to take appropriate spare parts and tools with him on the call.

With experience too, the engineer learns how different customers behave, and is able to predict how customers will react to equipment malfunction, and how they are likely to react to delays in restoring equipment to good working order.

When an engineer is assigned to a territory, he should draw up a simple three column grid. A card index system is useful. Alternatively an indexed exercise book can be used. The table below illustrates the grid. Column one shows the type of customer. Column two describes the customer operation. Column three puts the customer in a particular problem category.

For example, the first two columns of the grid are completed using the customer categories for an office photocopying machine.

Customer category	Operation	Problem category
● Large office	Equipment used continuously by many unskilled operators. Much opportunity for machine abuse.	
● Multinational company	Choice of equipment is dictated by overseas head office of company. Management resents their choice of equipment.	
● Copy shops	Profitability is prime consideration of operators. machine dead time is unacceptable and grudged. Recompense against machne failure often sought.	
● Walk-up site	Very heavy traffic from skilled and unskilled users.	
● Dedicated operators	Operator making constant use of equipment begins to assume infallible total knowledge. Has tendency to diagnose causes of	

	machine malfunction and tell the engineer what to do.
● Printers	Large throughput. Machine dead time must be kept to a minimum.
● Legal printers	As for printers but additionally copy quality must be immaculate.
● Colleges/ hospitals/ universities	Massive throughput. Skilled and unskilled operators.
● Civil service	Large throughput. Decision making in respect of repairs and purchases sometimes difficult.

The third column is completed by the engineer after he has called on site. The different types of problem category are now given, with a description of each type:

Problem category

● Awkward customers	Belligerent, egocentric and unhelpful. Extreme care is essential.
● Technology scared customers	Customers react to the slightest malfunction by calling for help. The simplest mechanical or technical activity is a mystery.
● Unskilled operators	Frequent machine abuse. Difficulties in changing from one operating mode to another lead to irritation and heavy machine handling.
● Copyshop moneymakers	In the context of busy work schedules, there is constant pressure to resolve machine downtime problems. Recompense for spoiled and wasted materials usually sought.
● Beleaguered secretary	The secretary is under constant pressure from above to make urgent

use of equipment. Consequently, she is inflexible in requirement for rapid and effective service.

● Trades Union run printers

Service engineers are not allowed to service or repair machine if not a member of appropriate union. Union tradesman has to be present to carry out particular aspect of repair relating to occupation.

● Offset replacers

Some offset litho printing workers have lost jobs due to installation of copying machines. Antagonism is expected – with little cooperation.

● 'What the salesman said'

What the salesman allegedly said is in conflict with the real situation. Diplomacy and authority are appropriate.

● 'What the other engineer said'

There is immediate conflict. The engineer must not blame his colleague. All relevant facts must be ascertained.

● 'What the company despatcher said'

It is with the despatcher that the client makes contact. Despatcher arranges for engineer to call. When appropriate, have recourse to despatcher. The prime objective is to rectify the problem.

SUMMARY

Question   **What is the role of the service engineer?**

Answer   The service engineer's role is to provide the efficient technical skills necessary to maintain company equipment.

Question What greeting does an engineer give on arrival at the customer's premises?

Answer The greeting to the customer at his premises should introduce the company and the engineer. An immediate request for problem-related information follows.

Question How should the engineer dress for visits to a customer's premises?

Answer If no uniform is provided the engineer should wear neat, unobtrusive but comfortable clothes.

Question What are the rules governing behaviour on the customer's premises?

Answer There are a number of Do's and Don'ts regarding the engineer's behaviour on site. They are designed to cause the least disturbance to the customer's activities and premises.

Question What should the engineer do when equipment abuse is diagnosed?

Answer When equipment abuse is diagnosed the engineer has two tasks to perform: 1 to restore the equipment to good working order; and 2 to provide immediate training in correct equipment operation.

Question What common pitfalls must engineers strive to avoid?

Answer Engineers must strenuously refrain from allocating blame for equipment malfunction.

Question What unmentionable things should be mentioned to the service engineer?

Answer The service engineer should take steps to avoid offending customers inadvertently through bad breath and bad body odours.

Question **What is the procedure for leaving a customer's premises after a service visit?**

Answer Before leaving, the engineer tidies away all related disturbance to customer's equipment and premises.

Question **What personal records are of practical use to the engineer?**

Answer A customer profile grid is of particular value to the engineer since it helps in the anticipation of customer equipment problems.

9 Turning complaints into orders

Before reading this chapter, try to answer the test questions given below. The answers will emerge in the chapter itself and appear in a summary at the end.

QUESTIONS

What two points are essentially being made by a customer who is complaining?

What makes a person buy?

What do service personnel need to know about the stages of making a buying decision, in order to turn a disgruntled person into a satisfied customer?

What is an important factor to remember in respect of every complaint received by the customer service department?

What approach is most helpful to the customer service department in turning complaints into orders?

Chapter 9 synopsis

● Why a customer complains
● How a buyer thinks
● How a seller sells
● Behind the customer complaint
● A set of useful rules

WHY A CUSTOMER COMPLAINS

Question   **What two points are essentially being made by a customer who is complaining?**

The variety of people in our society is very wide. Some cope adequately with the stresses and pressures of ordinary everyday life. Some fail. Others bulldoze their way through every challenge.

Management, concerned with customer service, doubtless believe that their contact is with a disproportionately large section of the strong and the articulate. Management know that those who do complain can sometimes be loud and tenacious, spiteful and self-seeking. The techniques, in training terms, for dealing with customer complaints are dealt with in detail in the next chapter. But the most important response to a complaint is to *listen*. Whether the customer is right or wrong the complaint, as defined by the customer, must be known.

The customer standing on his or her rights, or imagined rights, calls out for attention and sympathy. For the customer it is a 'them and us' situation. Although it may not be apparent from a restrained and modest approach, the customer can be drawing on considerable emotional reserves to help him state his case. Not everyone finds it easy to argue and dispute, and sympathetic attention can ease the way for the customer stating the problem.

Whether or not the customer complaint is valid, the customer believes that it is. From the customer's point of view, all is not right. This is an opportunity for service personnel, thinking as a salesman thinks, to sell benefits to the customer to make everything right.

HOW A BUYER THINKS

Question **What makes a person buy?**

People turn into customers, or are turned by salesmen into customers, because they have certain needs that must be satisfied.

Needs are essential requirements. They have to be fulfilled for the potential customer to go about his or her daily business in the most satisfactory way. Take an everyday item such as a coat. In the case of a postman, a coat is a necessity for carrying out his job. The prime needs of a person whose work involves much walking or cycling out of doors, such as a postman, might be classified as:

1 protection from the weather
2 warmth
3 durability.

The postman may also want the coat to be:

1 elegant
2 fashionable.

For example, he may want to wear a sheepskin coat with a lined hood. He may want others to see that the coat is expensive and fashionable. This want is a desire. It is something that the postman would like to have. The want, however, is not a real need.

The needs and wants of the fashion editor of a glossy magazine, as far as a coat is concerned, are different. Her needs are that the coat is:

1 fashionable
2 elegant.

Her wants are that the coat is warm. It is unlikely that durability is a feature, either as a need or a want.

Analysis of the buying process shows that decisions to purchase are made when:

1 some or all of the needs are satisfied
2 some or all of the wants are satisfied.

But the second situation is less common. A customer sometimes buys, acting on impulse, when the wants only are satisfied. The customer is much more likely to buy when the needs are met. Satisfaction of needs is provided by means of benefit messages and these are passed by the sales representative to the customer. Sometimes the customer perceives them spontaneously. There is no set format for a benefit message. It can be verbal, or visual, but can also be perceived by touch, sound, taste or smell. Benefit messages are frequently direct and to the point. For example, the coat salesman says to the postman: 'This coat is waterproof and very warm. It wears very well and will last you a long time'.

In making the statement the salesman is satisfying the needs of proof against the weather, warmth and durability. The statement is unlikely, however, to be effective in generating a buying decision from the fashion editor. It does not relate to her needs.

There are techniques that salesmen adopt to pass benefit messages. Indeed professional selling has an armoury of techniques that work. They are the tools of the trade, in the same way that every industry develops appropriate professional skills.

The most important aspect of a benefit message is that it refers to the *function* of a product or service, not the intrinsic features. The postman's coat sells because it is warm and weatherproof. The grading of the yarn and the numbers of warp and weft threads have little or no influence on the purchase decision.

HOW A SELLER SELLS

Question **What do service personnel need to know about the stages of making a buying decision, in order to turn a disgruntled person into a satisfied customer?**

In the decision making process of buying there are seven separate stages. But not everyone who reaches the decision to purchase starts from the same point. Some are well on the way to the 'decide to buy' stage. In such cases the task of the salesman whose objective is to influence the buying decision is easier.

Figure 9.1 illustrates the sequence of stages in a buying decision.

		Stage	
I am me. Respect me.	1	No interest	
What is this I see?	2	Casual interest	
Do I need it? Do I want it?	3	Motivated interest	
Shall I search for something different?	4	Shopping comparisons	
Where can I buy what I need?	5	Selection commitment	
I am going to buy. I feel good.	6	BUYING DECISION	
Oh, dear! Did I make the right decision?	7	Post-purchase doubts	

Figure 9.1 Sequence of stages in a buying decision

Stage	Sales technique
1 No interest 2 Casual interest	Attention getting.
3 Motivated interest	Qualifying through questions. The sales presentation.
4 Shopping comparisons	Objection handling.
5 Selection commitment	Benefit messages. Trial close.
6 BUYING DECISION	The close.
7 Post-purchase doubts	Reinforcement benefit messages.

Figure 9.2 Sales techniques and stages of the buying decision

A professional salesman, good at his job, is able in one meeting to move a potential customer through all the stages from 'no interest' to 'buy'. It does not happen all the time, but the better the salesman, the more often he succeeds. There is no reason why others, trained in different fields, cannot have the same success. It is necessary to learn the selling skills, and how to apply them.

Figure 9.2 shows the sales techniques necessary to move a prospective buyer through the successive stages.

Sales techniques

Attention getting. Initial contact is most courteous and polite. The successful salesman is careful of how he speaks. He dresses neatly. He presents his company and himself in a manner designed to impress. If any pre-established bonds exist, he uses them.

Qualifying through questions. Skilful use of open, closed and leading questions can find out almost anything. The salesman probes to identify the potential buyer's real needs. When these are known, the presentation is most effective because it is made in a way that matches benefit functions to the buyer's needs as closely as possible.

The sales presentation. A professional presentation describes, highlights, magnifies and promises everything that the product or service does. The spoken word is reinforced by illustration, by demonstration, by touch – and where appropriate by taste and smell too.

Those qualities of the product, the product benefits, that are nearest to what the customer wants are singled out. For example, the car dealer reinforces the carrying capacity of a motor car, when selling to a farmer. He gives preference to this product benefit over any others, although there are alternative product benefits, such as speed or status, which are good selling points to different buyers.

Objection handling. There are many, many reasons why people do not buy – insufficient money, lack of authority, fear of making a decision or ignorance of product features. Often the reason is simply inertia.

If the salesman is to close a sale he must overcome all objections. The objection that is given is not necessarily the most important one. For example: 'No. I don't like the colour. We will leave it, thank you'.

Perhaps the product is too expensive. The potential customer does not want to say this. He or she does not want to admit in public that they cannot afford something. If the salesman knows the real objection, his job is to help the customer overcome it. For example, if expense is the main objection, hire purchase arrangements, deferred terms, leasing, or, perhaps, a similar but less sophisticated product are all alternative options that can lead to a sale.

Armed with questions, to find out why there is resistance to buying, the seller has to produce persuasive counter-arguments to all the objections. The counter-arguments are most effectively based on product benefits.

Benefit messages. The benefit message is a statement of what the product can do for the buyer. It gives hope and promise.

Trial close. Throughout a sales presentation a good salesman continuously solicits signposts that he is moving in the right direction. 'Do you like it?' 'Will the equipment improve the production rate?' 'Do you like the colour?' 'Is the quoted price within your budget range?'

Every *yes* that is given reinforces the move towards the final close. If the question receives a *no*, the salesman has to consolidate his position. The trial close is a method of testing the water without placing the salesman in a position from which it is difficult to recover.

The close. When a presentation is closed successfully, a sale is achieved. The most effective method of closing is to ask for an order. It is essential, however, when this close is adopted, that the salesman does not say another word, until an answer is given. Weak salesmen crumple when they ask for an order directly. Because they worry that the answer is going to be no, they follow up the close request 'Will you authorise delivery?' with additional benefits. The moment additional words are spoken, the buyer is let off the hook.

After a request to buy, there is silence. The longer the silence continues, the harder it is for the buyer to say no. It is

difficult for the salesman too, who does not want to lose the
sale, but it is essential that he does not say a word.

Two words are to be avoided during a close: 'buy' and 'sign'.
They are both emotive. With many people, they generate
protective mechanisms that make the task of closing even
harder. 'Authorise' or 'order' are substitute words for 'buy'.
'Authorise' or 'write your signature' replace the word 'sign'.

Reinforcement benefit message. After a buying commitment,
many people wish that they had not made the decision. They
bring back the arguments against buying that they had considered before. Perhaps there are additional arguments against
buying, that had not been thought of previously.

Advertising copy in the media helps to dispel post-purchase
doubts. The authority of the printed message is comforting. A
good salesman reinforces the sale achieved, as hard as he can,
by pumping in additional benefit messages, even when the
signed contract is in his hand.

If a buyer really wants to change his mind after making a
commitment there are a few options open:

1   Ask the seller to release the contract or order.
Whether agreement is given to the request depends on the circumstances. A regular customer, or one who is potentially a source
of good business is likely to be allowed to change his mind.

2   Buy a release from the contract by paying a penalty.
There is no fixed amount. It is a matter of negotiation between
buyer and seller.

3   Find deliberate fault with the product so that the merchan-
dise can be rejected.
The product is examined in minute detail to find grounds for
rejection. It is not unknown for damage to be wilfully caused
to find a reason for complaint.

BEHIND THE CUSTOMER COMPLAINT

Question   What is an important factor to remember in respect of every complaint received by the customer service
department?

When countering the onslaught of an aggrieved customer, there is little time to philosophise on customer motivation. One is governed by the specific objective of satisfying the customer's urgent needs. The complaint is an immediate, but transient hurdle to be overcome.

Frequently, overcoming the customer complaint is regarded as an end in itself. But more can be achieved. Gentle selling tactics need to be applied. The customer is at stage 3 (motivated interest) of the buying decision process. If no pressure at all is applied the customer slips back to stage 1 (no interest).

The appropriate sales technique is 'qualifying through questions'. What is it that the customer really needs? Example: Customer complaint is that the ordered supply of continuous computer stationery is late in arriving. Computer printouts are stopped completely pending promised delivery. Questioning identifies that supplies are always ordered on an *ad hoc* basis when the operator notices that supplies are low. Business comes in small quantities intermittently, in the form of a telephone call from the operator.

The customer has a basic need, namely to have a supply of continuous computer stationery. This was identified by the company salesman before the account was opened. The need was matched with an offer to supply such paper and an order was placed. The need is still there, but it has changed. It has increased. Demand for the product using the paper has increased.

A few neutral leading questions identify the increased need. The rest of the sales cycle is straightforward. A main hurdle of product acceptance has already been overcome, so there is unlikely to be much resistance. The customer is currently buying the product, has repeated the order and knows the intrinsic product benefits. In the buying decision process the customer is ready to be moved along to stage 5 (selection commitment). Benefit messages support the sales presentation of increasing the order size. The customer should carry a buffer stock, so that computer printout downtime is avoided. There may be objections which are likely to be logistical. For example, the operator is not authorised to make purchases independently above a certain budget figure. With initiative such objections can mostly be overcome. The situation is very different from that in which a salesman is attempting to close an initial sale, and the objections given are not the real ones.

A close – the sales technique for stage 6 – should lead to a buying decision. Stage 7, post-purchase doubts, are unlikely to occur. They relate most frequently to purchases of consumer durables and capital goods.

A SET OF USEFUL RULES

Question **What approach is most helpful to the customer service department in turning complaints into orders?**

Complaints cannot always be turned into orders – but sometimes they can. Success is only achieved if an attempt is made. The worst that can happen is for the customer to say 'No'. The following rules summarise the route to gaining the extra orders:

Rules for turning complaints into orders

1 Listen
2 Deal with particular complaint appropriately
3 Question customer to identify (a) the original needs that are being satisfied by the company product or service, and (b) current needs that may be different from the original
4 Present new sales offer sandwiched between additional benefits to the customer
5 Counter objections
6 Close new business.

SUMMARY

Question **What two points are essentially being made by a customer who is complaining?**

Answer A person making a complaint really says two things, (1) I want attention and respect, and (2) I have unsatisfied needs.

Question **What makes a person buy?**

Answer In simple terms a person buys a product or service because he or she believes that it offers a means to improvement or pleasure.

Question **What do service personnel need to know about the stages of making a buying decision, in order to turn a disgruntled person into a satisfied customer?**

Answer In order to sell benefits and close a sale, it is helpful to be familiar with all the stages of the purchasing decision – from no interest through to buying commitment.

Question **What is an important factor to remember in respect of every complaint received by the customer service department?**

Answer An important factor to remember is that, before making a complaint, the customer needs have not been satisfied by the company.

Question **What approach is most helpful to the customer service department in turning complaints into orders?**

Answer A set of simple rules covering selling techniques is an effective guide to turning complaints into orders.

10 How to shoot trouble

Before reading this chapter, try to answer the test questions given below. The answers will emerge in the chapter itself and appear in a summary at the end.

QUESTIONS

What are the two areas of most concern to the customer service department troubleshooter?

What is the most serious customer problem met by the company troubleshooter?

Is a customer ever expendable?

What are the implications of disruption amongst service department personnel?

What format should the grievance interview take?

In what circumstances does a troubleshooter initiate action in respect of company employees?

What are the weapons of a troubleshooter in a disciplinary interview?

Chapter 10 synopsis

- Sources of trouble
- Difficult customers
- When the customer is wrong
- Trouble in the house
- How to settle grievances
- Settling company disturbances
- The troubleshooter's strengths

SOURCES OF TROUBLE

Question **What are the two areas of most concern to the customer service department troubleshooter?**

Customers are the lifeblood of any company and while they may not always be right, they must be treated as such. Sometimes customers are angry, belligerent, spiteful or even vicious. On rare occasions all these descriptions apply.

If the customer is not treated in a manner that he considers acceptable the business that he or she places may be lost. The lost business in itself is not always significant, but the damage to the company has a knock-on effect. A noisy altercation is embarrassing to members of staff, and also to nearby customers. The tensions thus created tend to linger.

Customers must be respected. They need to be wooed and cosseted. Anything that disrupts a rewarding reciprocal relationship between the company and the customer has to be swiftly put right.

Similarly, good morale amongst staff is essential to the corporate health of the company. Disruptive influences to morale and performance must be dealt with, and the person to do it is the troubleshooter. The action of troubleshooting can be carried out by anyone with the necessary qualifications, which are authority and judgement.

DIFFICULT CUSTOMERS

Question **What is the most serious customer problem met by the company troubleshooter?**

In every business, at some time, there are angry customers. There must therefore be a standardised response for dealing with such customers that all personnel are trained to use. The formula is a simple set of rules:

Rules for dealing with angry customers

1 *Listen*
Say nothing until the customer has stated his or her grievance. Do not interrupt!

2 *Sympathise*
The customer wants attention and respect, so give it. Commiserate and apologise. There need be no loss of dignity in giving sympathy and respect to an aggrieved customer.

3 *Establish the reason why the customer is angry*
Is the company at fault? Is the product wrong? Have company personnel offended the customer? Whether or not the complaint is justified, obtaining precise information is essential. More than likely, the necessary information has already been given by the customer. After the problem has been resolved it is important to make sure that it does not occur again.

4 *Take action to resolve the customer's problem*
The most practical steps and the quickest steps are the ones to take.

5 *Give the customer your name. Give the customer your commitment to resolving his or her problem*
Personal attention to a customer's needs cements good customer relations. It also repairs a relationship that has been disrupted.

6 *Follow up the action if any delay is scheduled*
It is necessary to make sure that promises and commitments are met.

When personnel cannot make an angry customer calm, even though the standard rules are applied, it is time for them to call on higher authority for help. Procedure should be standard. It can even be formulated as an additional rule.

7 *Call on management for help with customers who stay angry*
The status adopted by the troubleshooter has to be authoritative and impressive. Everything that contributes to credibility

is important. The angry customer is marginally happier speaking to a Director of Corporate Service Relations than to a supervisor even though the person is actually the same. Status alone, however creative, does not solve customer problems. But it is a starting point in troubleshooting.

WHEN THE CUSTOMER IS WRONG

Question **Is a customer ever expendable?**

Treating the customer as top priority is essential for company progress. There does, however, come a point when individual customers are expendable. Such decisions rest on the troubleshooter. Goodwill and future business are balanced against cost in real terms. Sometimes a longstanding relationship exists which is accompanied by goodwill, so decision making is not always easy. The following checklist provides guidelines to the troubleshooter in deciding what to do with the disruptive customer.

Checklist for dealing with disruptive customers

Place tick in appropriate box   YES   NO

- If the present incident is resolved in a manner acceptable to the customer, is the future relationship likely to be trouble free?   ☐   ☐

- Should tolerance be shown towards the customer on the grounds of good business transacted in the past?   ☐   ☐

- Should tolerance be shown to the customer on the grounds of projected future business?   ☐   ☐

- Is an additional effort appropriate to mollify and make peace with the customer?   ☐   ☐

- From the customer point of view, is the complaint reasonable?   ☐   ☐

- Is there evidence that future business is likely to follow from meeting the customer complaint?   ☐   ☐

- Objectively, can the company's activities be described as flexible and fair?   ☐   ☐

- Does the company realistically want to retain the customer as a customer?   ☐   ☐

- Will a severance of the relationship with the customer react adversely on
a   other customers,   ☐   ☐
b   company personnel?   ☐   ☐

- Can the financial cost of meeting and resolving the customer's complaint be offset against current profits?   ☐   ☐

- Is it possible for the personnel involved with the customer to make a greater effort at resolving differences?   ☐   ☐

If the answers are Yes, greater effort should be made to satisfy the customer and endeavour to retain the business. If No is the answer to more than two questions, serious consideration is appropriate for severing the relationship.

TROUBLE IN THE HOUSE

Question **What are the implications of disruption amongst service department personnel?**

There is a hierarchy in the factors disturbing personnel in their work. The starting point is dissatisfaction.

Dissatisfaction	This is any factor disturbing an employee, irrespective of whether or not it has been expressed.
Complaint	A dissatisfaction that is spoken or written.

Grievance   A complaint that has been
                               formally presented to
                               management, or to a union
                               official if appropriate.

If a complaint is not made, management is not always aware
that dissatisfaction exists. It may shrug off an odd disruption
or disturbance. But when a complaint has been made, there is
something positive to account for a deterioration in service.

It is the service manager's task to assume the role of troubleshooter. The task is not always straightforward. A complaint
is an indication that there is some form of trouble. It is not
always clear what the real trouble is. A complaint can be
likened to the objection given by a potential customer to a
salesman. It is an objection, but it is not the real one. For
example, the complaint states that it is cold in the storeroom.
The real complaint is that the storeroom manager appears to
dislike and pick on the person making the complaint.

It may be that domestic or marital problems place undue
stress on a service engineer, and this can affect performance.
For instance, an engineer concerned over a baby's health and
anxious to be at home may shirk duties that are otherwise
willingly undertaken.

Complaints and dissatisfaction are symptoms. Grievances
are causes. From the symptoms the troubleshooter must probe
to find and deal with the true underlying causes of the complaint and disturbance. When the problem has not reached the
formal stage of the grievance, it can be dealt with informally.
Personnel whose performance is giving cause for concern can
be counselled over a drink in a pub, or coffee in the canteen.
Care must be taken, however, in giving advice and judgement
on personal matters. If an opinion is requested, it can be given
as a personal opinion. Alternatively, consultation can be sug-
gested with the person's doctor or with the Citizens' Advice
Bureau. On matters that relate to the company and to the
individual's performance, advice and direction must certainly
be given. A manager's guidance and control is a form of
security. It gives stability to those in his or her department.

The lodging of a formal grievance calls for a formal response. Records are kept of the grievance and the outcome
in the personal file of the individual or persons concerned.

Grievances are dealt with at a grievance interview, where the procedure is planned and businesslike.

HOW TO SETTLE GRIEVANCES

Question **What format should the grievance interview take?**

The following are guidelines for conducting the grievance interview:

Rules for conducting the grievance interview

Rule 1　Arrange the location

An office or interview room is appropriate. If the interview is held in the local pub, the employee may feel that it does not really count. A specific time set for interview on company business premises reinforces the view that the matter is being taken seriously.

Rule 2　State the grievance that has been lodged

There are two reasons for this. First, the employee hears the grievance out of context, removed from his or her present train of thought. The procedure is the same as that used by a salesman in countering a customer's objection to a sale being closed. The objection is repeated by the salesman for the customer to hear. Secondly, it summarises the position as understood by the manager at the outset of the interview.

Rule 3　Invite the employee to confirm that his or her case has been correctly stated

There are sometimes difficulties. Employees can be apprehensive. In their grievance they may be questioning the authority of management. Often they are not skilled in stating their case as they see it. Far from being articulate and aggressive they are tongue-tied and stumble in explaining their meaning.

Rule 4 Do not interrupt

It is best to save all questions for the end. Interruptions can increase the difficulties of a poorly presented case.

Rule 5 Do not argue

Arguments can lead to a stalemate. 'Yes I did' against 'No you did not'. This direct confrontation is a dead end and an obstacle to a solution of the problem.

Rule 6 Restate the complaint

After questions and answers to clarify any outstanding points, the position should be clear. The restatement is a summary.

Rule 7 Resolve the problem

A solution is necessary for the problem underlying the grievance.

Rule 8 Do not make promises that cannot be kept

Solutions are not always easy, or even possible. Promises are a temporary solution, but they must be supportable. Where solutions are not possible, the grievance interview itself has a contribution that is in some way therapeutic. The interview means that the company does listen and does care.

SETTLING COMPANY DISTURBANCES

Question **In what circumstances does a troubleshooter initiate action in respect of company employees?**

Management dissatisfaction rather than employee dissatisfaction are the circumstances for troubleshooting action that lead to a disciplinary interview.

The interview is a considered step. Many companies draw up a sequence of actions for disciplinary procedure. If there are unions within the workforce, the procedure is likely to have been negotiated and agreed with them. When procedures exist, they must be followed. Procedures take the following form:

Typical company disciplinary procedure

Step 1   Give a warning

Warnings are never given in front of the employee's colleagues. The warning can be verbal or in writing, but must state what circumstances are infringed and the behaviour expected from the employee. It is usual for the manager to take the employee aside. For the initial warning a full disciplinary interview is not always necessary.

Step 2   Hold disciplinary interview

The management objective is to eradicate indiscipline. The options are, (a) give a second warning setting out the precise penalty actions contingent on further misdemeanour and (b) impose penalty actions.

Details of penalty actions imposed are recorded in writing and handed to the employee. A copy is handed to the union representative. Note that disciplinary action should not be taken against a shop steward without prior discussion with a senior official of the union involved.

Step 3   Implement penalty action

Penalty actions come into force if breaches of discipline occur after the second warning, or if sufficiently serious, after the first warning has been given. Whatever the penalty the dignity of the employee must be left intact.

THE TROUBLESHOOTER'S STRENGTHS

Question What are the weapons of a troubleshooter in a disciplinary interview?

Breaches of discipline arise for a number of reasons:

(1) Ignorance. Company procedures are not known.

(2) Inadequate training. The implications of some safety regulations are contingent upon training and experience.
(3) Inertia. Lack of motivation to meet the set requirements.
(4) Wilful lack of concern. The employee has no interest in conforming to disciplinary strictures.

In the disciplinary interview the task of the troubleshooter is to achieve a change of behaviour. It is necessary that the employee knows precisely what is required of him or her and makes a commitment to that change. Attitudes antagonistic to discipline must also be changed. The following rules provide a structure for the disciplinary interview:

Rules governing the disciplinary interview

Rule 1   State the management view of the breach of discipline

The statement must be factual, such as, a company vehicle has persistently been used for personal activities in breach of company regulations. The opinion of the manager that the employee is an unreliable cheat for using the vehicle is not appropriate.

In fact, there may be extenuating medical grounds for the action. Management's statement of the facts of the case must be comprehensive. The employee has to know the full extent of management dissatisfaction, and the reasons that apply.

Rule 2   Invite employee's explanation for the breach of discipline

One of three circumstances applies:
(a)   a straightforward response is given
(b)   the employee is withdrawn, and apprehensive
(c)   there is aggressive defiance
In the second circumstance the manager needs to probe with open and leading questions to find the underlying cause. The actual reason may be a cause of embarrassment or distress to the employee.

In the last situation controlled logic and calmness are the best counter to employee hostility.

Rule 3   Seek a solution to the cause of the problem

If the problem that causes a breach of discipline is readily solved, there is an early end to the disciplinary interview. There are three approaches:

(a) Persuasion. Achieve a change of attitude by persuasion. 'Promotion next year could be considered, if the attendance sheet showed a marked improvement.'

(b) Disapproval. Achieve a commitment to improved performance by the disapproval of those whose opinions the employee values. 'Your parents would be horrified if they heard of your brutal behaviour.'

(c) Penalties. The ultimate reaction to persistent lack of discipline. Penalties can take the form of a fine, or loss of amenities. In grave circumstances summary dismissal is possible.

Rule 4 Implement the action that follows from Rule 3

Rule 5 Prepare a written record of the interview

Give one copy to the employee, one copy to the union representative. Place the record in the personal employee file.

Rule 6 Review employee performance

After a period of one month, review performance to see whether the employee now conforms to the standards of performance or behaviour required. In many companies, provision is made to 'forget' disciplinary proceedings once a prescribed period of blameless performance and behaviour has been achieved.

SUMMARY

Question What are the two areas of most concern to the customer service department troubleshooter?

Answer Customers and departmental personnel are the two areas where trouble must be resolved promptly and firmly.

Question What is the most serious customer problem met by the company troubleshooter?

Answer The most serious customer problem is that of the angry disruptive customer.

Question Is a customer ever expendable?

Answer Disruptive customers are a liability. It rests on the discretion of the troubleshooter when such customers can no longer be supported.

Question What are the implications of disruption amongst service department personnel?

Answer Disruption amongst departmental personnel indicates that there is dissatisfaction. The reasons for the dissatisfaction may not be known.

Question What format should the grievance interview take?

Answer Conducted in a formal setting, the grievance interview identifies and clarifies the underlying causes of the employee grievance, and endeavours to find a solution.

Question In what circumstances does a troubleshooter initiate action in respect of company employees?

Answer A troubleshooter initiates action when management is dissatisfied with performance and behaviour.

Question What are the weapons of a troubleshooter in a disciplinary interview?

Answer In a disciplinary interview a troubleshooter has recourse to persuasion, disapproval, penalties and dismissal from the company.

Further reading

'Working for Customers', CBI, Oct. 1983.

Pat Clayton, *Law for the Small Business*, Kogan Page, 1979.

Donald Cowell, *The Marketing of Services*, Heinemann, 1984.

Goode, R. M. (ed.), *Commercial Law Statutes*, Sweet & Maxwell, 1979.

Bernard Katz, 'When customers ring your company for service, what do they expect?', *Industrial Marketing Digest*, Vol. 9/4–1984.

Bernard Katz, *How to Win more Business by Phone*, Business Books, 1983.

Lowe, R. and Woodroffe, G., *Consumer Law and Practice*, Sweet and Maxwell, 1980.

John M. Rathmell, *Marketing in the Service Sector*, Winthrop Publishers Inc., 1974.

Stone, M. and Wild, A., *Field Service Management*, Gower, 1985.

Derek Torrington and John Chapman, *Personnel Management*, Prentice-Hall International.

John H. Wellemin, *Professional Service Management*, Chartwell-Bratt Ltd., 1984.

Michael Whincup, *Product Liability Law*, Gower, 1985.

James R. H. White, *Successful Supervision*, McGraw-Hill.

Index